not your mama's™ *felting*

The cool and creative way to get it together

by Amy Swenson

For general information on our other products and services or to obtain technical support please contact our Customer Care Department within the U.S. at (800) 762-2974, outside the U.S. at (317) 572-3993 or fax (317) 572-4002.

Wiley also publishes its books in a variety of electronic formats. Some content that appears in print may not be available in electronic books. For more information about Wiley products, please visit our web site at www.wiley.com.

Library of Congress Cataloging-in-Publication Data:

Swenson, Amy, 1977-
Not your mama's felting : the cool and creative way to get it together / by Amy Swenson.
    p. cm. — (Not your mama's)
  ISBN-13: 978-0-470-09518-8 (pbk.)
  ISBN-10: 0-470-09518-0
  1. Felt work.   2. Felting   I. Title.
  TT849.5.S94   2007
  746'.0463—dc22
                                        2006101038
Printed in the United States of America

10 9 8 7 6 5 4 3 2 1

Book design by Elizabeth Brooks
Cover design by Troy Cummings
Interior photography by Matt Bowen
Illustrations by Joni Burns, Shelley Norris, Rashell Smith, Jake Mansfield
Book production by Wiley Publishing, Inc. Composition Services
Wiley Bicentennial Logo: Richard J. Pacifico

This book is dedicated to Boo, my darling baby cat,
who napped on the piles of merino fiber while I was hard at work.

Free bonus pattern available online!

Can't get enough felting? Access one more *Not Your Mama's Felting* pattern at www.wiley.com/go/notyourmamas.

Contents

PART TWO
Patterns and Projects

CHAPTER SIX

Never Too Many Bags

CHAPTER SEVEN

Stuff to Wear

CHAPTER EIGHT

Quick Gifts & Oddities

CHAPTER NINE

Cozy Felt for Your Home

Acknowledgments

To the great folks at Wiley, who are probably quite sick of me after working on two books, back-to-back, thank you for your advice, assistance, and general whipping-me-into-shape. Mandy Moore and Edie Eckman deserve special acknowledgment for doing a stellar job on the technical editing of the content and the patterns in this book. Huge thank you's are also owed to all the fascinating fiber artists who I encounter every day at Make One Yarn Studio. Your creativity is a constant source of inspiration. My partner Sandra couldn't have anticipated how much this book would consume not only my life, but also our kitchen, backyard, and basement. Months after the projects have all been finished, and the supplies have been moved back into the studio, we're still finding bits of fleece and abandoned felt everywhere.

Introduction

◆◆◆

Get Felt Up and Full of It!

Do you want to try out the world's oldest textile art? How about taking your knitting or crochet to new and crazy places? Do you love the smell of wet sheep? Do you already know that wet alpaca is one of the worst stinks aside from a durian fruit?

Whatever your reasons for picking up this book, I'm so glad you did.

You see, magical things happen when you mix hot water and wool. You can make sheer, lightweight scarves and shawls. You can make the coziest of blankets or warm woolen mittens. You can turn a simple knit sack into a delightfully strong and water-resistant bag. Yes, these *are* a few of my favorite things.

I'm guessing you picked up this book because you're curious. Maybe you've already knit and *felted* a few things. Or maybe the clueless laundry dolt in your life has inadvertently felted your best sweater in the washing machine. Maybe, you're a dedicated lover of art and saw an exhibit on felted sculpture. Or maybe you're just looking for something new.

Whether you've come to this book on the rebound or because you're already well enchanted with the idea of felting, I hope you find some inspiration and fun in the following chapters.

How to Use This Book

Not Your Mama's Felting is designed for anyone from crafting novices to Martha Stewart-worthy experts. No matter how many felting projects you've worked in the past, you're likely to find something new within the next 200 or so pages.

The first part of the book, chapters 1 through 5, teaches you most of the essentials: all about fiber, wet felting, needle felting, fulling, and dyeing. In the second part, you'll dig into some incredible, fashionable, and fun patterns that your mama will be jealous of. For felting fans, both new and true, the third part of this book gives all the geeky details for where to go next.

You'll notice that the patterns and projects in this book cover knitting, crochet, sewing, wet felting, and needle felting. Even within each of the skills, we've included a range of projects to suit any skill level. If you've done knitting or crochet before, you'll notice we left off any difficulty ratings. It's my belief that there are no easy or hard felting patterns. Instead, our ratings are done based on time commitment.

- ♦ Flirtation These projects are quick, easy, and great for experimentation.
- ♦ Summer Fling Takes a bit more time and more concentration, but still has a fair amount of instant gratification.
- ♦ Love o' Your Life Ready for commitment? Like the best relationships, you'll put a lot of work in but get a lot of enjoyment (or bragging rights) out of the final product.

In the mood for a one-nighter? Look for projects labeled "Flirtation" and you'll be done during a single chick flick. "Summer Fling" projects take a little longer. These might be better for Christmas vacation or a week at the beach. "Love o' Your Life" are the sort of projects you'll labor long for. These might take a month or more, but at the end, you'll have a true heirloom.

Each of the projects also includes a suggested variation. Use these as a jumping off point for your own experiments! Instead of just substituting yarn or switching up the color, these ideas should help you make some creative decisions to make the project your own.

Feel Like Makin' Felt . . .

I confess. Not long ago, I thought that the only type of felting was when I'd knit a big bag and shrink it in the washing machine. I suppose that deep down, I knew that boiled wool jackets had to be created with a somewhat different process, that the wool felt blankets and other ancient artifacts on display in history museums were probably not fresh off the knitting needles. And, I also knew that needle felting was something different altogether.

But, as it turns out, traditional felt making has nothing to do with yarn at all. Instead, raw, un-spun wool is laid out into the desired shape, and then hot soapy water and friction are applied to mat and shrink the fiber together until a cohesive fabric forms. How novel! How speedy! I could make a scarf in an hour, a throw blanket in three. Knitting would never be so fast!

And so, the love affair began. Although my first love is yarn and everything that can be done with it, I don't feel guilty cheating on my knitting with these interludes of felt. Felting gives a hands-on instant gratification that also connects me to the very first fiber artists, 10,000 years ago. It allows for creativity in a completely different way than knitting or crochet, and it lets me create garments and accessories that are sculptural, soft, and completely cuddly.

But of course, fulling—or shrinking—a knit, woven, or crocheted fabric, is equally enchanting. When else can you knit a bag that's bigger than your cat and have it end up the perfect size for Friday nights on the town? When else can you produce something that looks so far removed from its original state that friends and loved ones refuse to believe you could actually make such a thing? How often do you really get to pull out those 10mm knitting needles or 15mm crochet hook?

Although the resulting fabric is similar to when felting with raw fleece and water, the fulling of a knit or crocheted fabric is a different process. You can do this step by hand in the kitchen sink, but yarnaholics just throw the item in the washing machine, set it to hot, and watch the magic happen.

• Part One •

How to Felt

Chapter One

◆◆◆

Your Daily Dose of Fiber

Fiber ain't just for breakfast!

To make felt—any kind of felt—you need some sort of yarn or fluffy stuff or fabric. The first pieces of felt ever made centuries ago were likely crafted from loose bits of sheep wool. Today, as the pages of this book will show, you can create felt from loose fiber (such as sheep's wool), yarn, old sweaters, and more. But first, you need to have an idea what kind of felting you are going to do, so you know what kind and form of fiber you need.

Felt Happens

No matter whether you're wet felting, needle felting, or fulling from an already created fabric, felt happens when friction is applied to a felt-able fiber. In most cases, soapy water significantly helps things along. Heat doesn't hurt, either. Water, soap, and heat all help to loosen up the fibers and help them to stick together. So, let's look at the different types of felting covered in this book, and why they work.

Wet Felting

Wet felting is achieved by carefully overlapping wool fiber in several perpendicular layers, then applying a bit of hot, soapy water and gently rubbing until the fibers interlock. Wet felting can be done flat or three-dimensionally on a solid form such as a bottle or jar. You can also create some neat effects by wet felting artfully arranged wool onto a porous fabric, such as silk chiffon or cheesecloth. Not to let anything constrain you, you can felt balls or ropes in your hands or felt around a piece of plastic to create pouches and bags. In all these cases, raw fiber is layered; then wet; then rubbed, pressed, or rolled until a cohesive, smooth, solid fabric forms. I cover wet felting in the following chapter. See some examples of wet felted scarves in chapter 7.

Needle Felting, or Dry Felting

The only form of waterless felting uses barbed needles to repeatedly puncture the wool fiber, in essence, attaching the fibers as if sewing without thread. Needle felting is a quick and clean (if slightly dangerous) way to appliqué onto wool fabric, perhaps an already felted bag? You can needle felt either fiber or yarn. Yarn works great for outlines or detail work, but unspun fiber is ideal for larger sections of color. In addition to applying detail to another object, needle felting works for three-dimensional objects. You'll read about needle felting in chapter 3. Check out the needle-felted flowers in chapter 8.

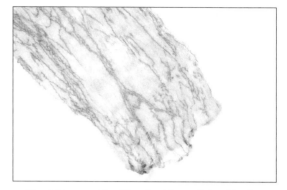

Wet felting; see Scarf for the Subzero Urban Dweller on page 129.

Needle felting; see Spring Is Sprung! on page 141.

Fulling (a.k.a. Felting a Fabric)

Most knitters and crocheters have seen this type of felting in their local yarn stores or favorite magazines. Yarn is knit or crocheted extremely loosely and shaped with the usual increases or decreases to create an object. Any individual pieces are sewn together loosely with the same yarn as the object. The whole thing is then thrown into the washing machine on a hot wash cycle with a little bit of detergent. After 5 minutes (or 50), the object has shrunk significantly, and individual stitches are no longer easy to spot. The fabric may get exceptionally bubbly or fuzzy, depending on the yarn used, and the type of washer.

Technically, this process isn't called felting at all . . . it's called *fulling*. Before you accuse this book of being totally full of it, or think that all those great felted bag patterns have it wrong, relax. I'll let you off the hook. The common crafter vocabulary is pretty set in calling this process *felting*. After all, the end result isn't that different looking than what you get from a half hour of wet felting a piece of fabric. It's just the process that differs.

For crafty guys and gals, it's probably most common to full a knitted or crocheted accessory. But, it's also easy to full woven fabrics or store-bought knit garments. Just make sure the fiber content is 100 percent non-superwash wool, or a blend of wool, mohair, angora, cashmere, and so on. You'll get more specifics on how to full in chapter 4.

Fulling; see Rainbow Bridge Baby Blanket on page 164.

Animal, Vegetable, or Mineral: Which Felts?

Any yarn or fiber addict knows that yarn comes in three main categories: man-made (acrylic, nylon, metallic), plant-based (cotton, linen, and hemp), and animal-produced. Although you can get some neat effects by incorporating synthetic or vegetable fibers in your felting projects, overall, you'll need fiber from an animal to successfully produce felt of any kind.

Traditionally, felt is made from the shorn wool of a sheep. But you can make felt from nearly any protein-based fiber that hasn't been treated with a chemical to make it shrink-resistant. Whether you choose fiber from a sheep, alpaca, rabbit, llama, cat, dog, or your own head (think dreadlocks), any fiber that originated from an animal should eventually felt—technically.

Every one of these fibers is covered with tiny overlapping scales. Just like the bits on a pinecone, these scales are attached only at one end, with the other end free. During the felting process, these scales will first swell with water to open outward, and then, as friction is applied, the scales will interlock, creating a dense fabric and appearing to shrink.

However, the fiber from each breed of animal has different properties. Expert felters and spinners of yarn will mention terms such as *crimp*—the waviness of the fiber—and *staple length*—the length of the average piece of fiber. But, as a novice felter, you don't need to be too concerned with the type-A technicalities. Knowing the different properties of the main types of feltable fiber will help your projects be as successful as possible.

Wool

Wool is the most common of the protein fibers. In many places, the words *wool* and *yarn* are actually used interchangeably. Wool is the final product of sheep fleece, shorn from the adult sheep, typically once a year. Hundreds of breeds of sheep can be found around the world, with each breed possessing different staple lengths, crimp, and colors of fleece.

In terms of felt-ability, the wool from some breeds of sheep felt more quickly and are easier to use than others, whether you are wet felting or using yarn to full a knitted or crocheted object. Merino is one of the most universally popular breeds of sheep. Exceptionally soft, merino is also extremely fast to felt. Some fiber artists joke that merino felts when you look at it cross-eyed. Luckily, merino is one of the most common types of raw fiber seen in your local supply store. It's also reasonably priced in undyed form. Fine merino yarn is also plentiful in most yarn stores. Just make sure that the yarn isn't labeled "Superwash." The care instructions, if any, should specify hand washing in cool water. Other good breeds for felting include Gotland, Blue Faced Leicester, and Rambouillet.

Mohair

Mohair is actually goat hair. Kid mohair is typically the softest, shorn from goats younger than 18 months. Adult mohair can vary from fine and lustrous to coarse and hairy. In yarn, you'll often see blends of wool and mohair. This allows the yarn to combine the halo and shine of the mohair with the density and elasticity of wool. Mohair/wool blended yarn is fantastic for felting. Some of the projects in this book use Brown Sheep Lamb's Pride yarn, an 85 percent wool / 15 percent mohair blend widely available in yarn shops and online. It creates a furry and dense felt compared to a straight wool and has a lovely shine. Needle felters can take advantage of pure mohair yarn for adding texture to any design. For wet felting, it's unusual to use straight mohair fiber, but it is possible. If this is of interest, experiment! You never know what will happen!

Cashmere, Angora, and Alpaca

Exotic fibers, including cashmere, angora, and alpaca, can be excellent substitutions for the more rough and hard-working wool.

Cashmere, from central Asian goats, is extremely soft and lightweight. It's also exceptionally pricey and fairly delicate. You wouldn't necessarily choose cashmere for a felted floormat, for example.

Angora is the downy coat of Angora rabbits, and is soft and silky. Pure angora fiber and yarn sheds quite a bit and may blow away in the breeze before you get a chance to begin felting. However, blends of angora and wool felt into a soft and downy fabric that's far lighter in weight than a straight wool garment would be. Check out the Cropped Cardigan pattern in chapter 7 to see how angora can be improved by felting!

In the past few years, alpaca has gotten to be nearly as widely available as wool. Without adding much expense, alpaca can provide some of the drape and loft of cashmere. Try felting with a pure alpaca yarn or fiber . . . you'll get a soft and slinky fabric that pure wool could never provide. One word of warning; wet alpaca is extremely stinky. Think "wet dog" but 10 times worse.

How to Buy Wool for Felting

Nearly all of the wet felting projects in this book use wool of some type. So, although the following information can also be applied to alpaca, cashmere, mohair, and other animal fibers, we'll try to keep things simple by just talking about wool.

Aside from yarn, which we'll cover later in the chapter, the fleece of a sheep can be purchased in many different forms; unprocessed fleece, batts, and combed roving.

Although it's unusual for a novice felter to go out and purchase a freshly sheared sheep fleece, it is possible to take the wool all the way from barnyard to runway. Unprocessed fleece hasn't even been cleaned. Giving it a good soak, wash, and deep cleaning is the first step to obtaining usable wool.

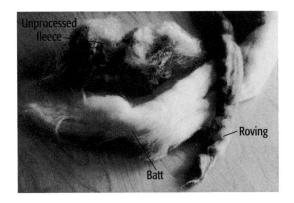

Next, the fleece will be combed or carded to make the fibers align in the same direction. Although you can do these things at home with a small amount of equipment, a decent amount of time, and a large willingness to get down and dirty, most hobby felters simply purchase wool that's already been cleaned and carded, and sometimes even dyed.

In the shop, look for bags labeled *top, sliver,* or *roving.* All these words generally mean that the fiber has been cleaned and combed so all pieces are facing the same direction. Wool that's been carded will look smooth to the eye and can usually be lifted out of the bag in one long rope-like piece. In contrast, you can also sometimes find wool *batts.* Batts are thin layers of carded wool that have been stacked atop each other. In the bag, a wool batt will look a lot like the acrylic poly-fil stuffing you can buy at your local craft store.

What Is This Stuff?

If you're extremely lucky, at some point a well-meaning friend or relative will gift you with unwanted yarn. Sometimes you'll be blessed with a very helpful label that details the fiber content of the yarn, the care instructions, the length, and the weight. Other times, you'll have to suss it out for yourself. The *melt test* has long been a quick and dirty method for narrowing down the options. Before trying this at home, you'll want to make sure you have a fireproof container, such as a large stock pot, and a set of metal tongs to hold the yarn, as well as a lighter or matches. While doing this, make sure to hold everything over the stock pot, so any stray ashes are contained. Take a lighter or match to the end of a piece of yarn and let it burn for a second before blowing it out. Is the odor chemical? Does the end of the yarn now contain a hard "bead?" If so, you have a synthetic yarn. If a fine ash forms and you smell burning paper, you're likely looking at cotton, linen or another cellulose fiber. If a crushable ash forms and you smell burning hair, you're blessed with a protein fiber of some kind.

Of course, many yarns are actually blends of one or more of these types. When using the melt test, the results will reflect the majority of the fiber. So, before knitting and attempting to felt a large project, you really should try knitting a small square out of the yarn to see how it felts. Of course, you should be doing this swatching anyway.

For needle felting projects, the type of wool doesn't much matter. But, for wet felting, you might find it easier to start from wool roving. Since the fibers in roving are clearly defined and aligned, it will make it that much easier to effectively set up your layers for felting.

All about Yarn

For projects that need to be knit or crocheted prior to fulling, you'll need some sort of yarn. As previously mentioned, this yarn needs to be shrinkable. So, cotton, linen, superwash wool, and anything with nylon or acrylic or rayon or silk can instantly be ruled out for most projects. Since most fulled projects are destined to be shrunk into a relatively smooth fabric, highly textured yarns can be overkill. . . the texture won't show in the end, anyway.

Yarn typically can be found everywhere from your local grocery store to high-end yarn boutiques. In general, it's tough, almost impossible, to find natural, shrinkable wool in large chain stores. For whatever reason, they tend to focus more on synthetic, easy-case yarns. Two exceptions to this rule are Patons Classic Merino Wool and Lion Brand Lion Wool. Either of these yarns can be found in many larger craft chain stores in Canada, the UK, and the USA, respectively. Look also at your local farmer's market for fresh-from-the-sheep wool yarns, often at inexpensive prices. For more tips on yarn shopping, check out chapter 11's section on "Stash Enhancing Fun."

Choosing the Perfect Fulling Yarn

Yarn selection has the most impact on the finished piece. Want a wild and furry piece of felt? Look for yarn with some mohair content. Want something smoother and more refined? Pure merino is the way to go. In your search for the perfect felting yarn for any given project, the possibilities may seem overwhelming. Here are a few of my favorite tips for choosing yarn.

Read the Ball Band

In many cases, your first clue that a pure wool yarn will felt are words on the ball band such as "Pure Virgin Wool," or "Organic Merino," or even instructions indicating that you should only hand wash in cool water. Fiber content indicating pure wool, or mixtures of wool and mohair, alpaca, cashmere, or angora will quite possibly full nicely. You'll still want to swatch for any yarn that doesn't come with a personal recommendation or wasn't specifically listed in a pattern. Some hand-dyed yarns or luxury yarns may direct you to hand wash only to preserve the color or texture of the yarn. These yarns have already been chemically treated to be shrink-resistant.

In no case should you buy a yarn labeled "Superwash." These yarns will not full, no matter how much time you spend on them. Also, until you're confidently experimenting with different fiber blends, avoid any yarn with a synthetic or plant-based content. The portions of the yarn containing the nylon, cotton, hemp, linen, or polyamide will not full, and the animal-based fibers may full only slightly. This can create a cool fabric, or it can just look like a mess. Read on for more tips on blends.

Some Favorite Felting Yarns

Although you've learned the short list of rules surrounding suitable fulling yarns, sometimes it helps to have a personal recommendation. The following is an incomplete list of some of my favorite, personally tested felting yarns. Any yarns on this list should full eventually. Just keep going! Have I left anything out? Absolutely! These are just yarns I can personally vouch for.

Alafoss Lopi and Lett Lopi
Blue Sky Alpaca Bulky
Blue Sky Alpaca Sport
Brown Sheep Lamb's Pride Worsted
Brown Sheep Lamb's Pride Bulky
Cascade 220
Cascade Pastaza
Colinette Point 5
Elann Peruvian Collection Highland Wool
Lion Brand Lion Wool
Lorna's Laces Fisherman

Lorna's Laces Bullfrogs & Butterflies
Malabrigo
Manos del Uruguay
Noro Kureyon
Noro Shinano
Patons Classic Merino Worsted
Rowan Big Wool
Rowan Felted Tweed
Schaefer Miss Priss
Schaefer Esperanza

Substitute Smartly

Although it's not always possible to obtain the yarn the pattern recommends, taking a closer look at the yarn can help make a more informed choice. Specifically, check out fiber content, thickness, and ply. The pattern should mention the fiber content of the original yarn, along with the length and physical weight of the ball or skein. For thickness, or weight of the yarn, you're looking for the typical gauge in knitted stocking stitch for a non-fulled project. Some patterns, including the ones in this book, provide this information. For others, ask at your local yarn shop or look the yarn up on Yarndex (www.yarndex.com), an online index of yarn information. Finally, ply matters! A loosely spun single-ply yarn may felt in a more wild or lumpy way than a smooth 4-ply. Again, Yarndex is a good resource for this kind of information.

Hanks, Balls, and Skeins, Oh My!

In cartoons, yarn always comes in perfect huge balls for kitten-chasing delight. In reality, yarn can be purchased in many forms.

Many yarn brands are sold in little cake or donut-shaped balls in 50g or 100g sizes. These balls, when the labels are removed, can easily be crocheted or knit directly from the center of

Pull-skeins

Balls

Hanks/skeins

the ball with no prep work required. As you work, the ball will empty from the center out. These are often called *center-pull ball*s.

Pull-skeins are similar to balls but shaped more like a log—long rather than round. As with center-pull balls, you can knit or crochet directly from the center of the pull-skein. Patons Classic Merino and Lion Brand Lion Wool are packaged as pull-skeins. Although you can find these beasts up to one-pounder sizes, it's rare to find a commercial feltable wool packaged that large. Noro Kureyon, for example, is packaged in a 50g pull-skein.

For both balls and pull-skeins, although the yarn is supposed to pull neatly from the center, you'll occasionally run into some tangles, especially near the beginning of the ball. Have patience—these are seldom actual knots. Using your fingers to gently jostle and loosen the fibers will help straighten out the yarn. Occasionally, the outside end is tucked into the center of the ball. Before digging around inside, make sure to pull out this outer tail.

Not to be confused with pull-skeins, the general terms *hank* and *skein* refer to the same packaging; a twisty-looking long object, not unlike a twisted pastry or roll. It's not uncommon, especially when buying pure wools from yarn shops or farm-fresh yarn from independent mills, to get yarn in skeins. With skeins, the producer has wound the yarn into a large ring, approximately 4 ft. in circumference, and tied it at several points. The skein is then folded in half, or twisted and wound into itself, and secured with a label. To use a skein of yarn, you'll need to first untwist it into a large ring, then wind a ball. There are special instruments for this task—swifts to hold the ring of yarn and ball winders with cranks to make a ball of yarn; however, draping the ring over your knees and using your hands to make a ball works just fine, too.

A Tangled Mess: How to Wind a Ball of Yarn

It happens to everyone at the beginning. That lovely length of yarn that came all twisted in a nice perfect hank becomes quickly tangled while beginning to work. Avoid this newbie trap by winding the yarn into a ball before you begin!

To wind a perfect ball of yarn from a skein, do the following:

1. Remove the label. Untwist the skein until you have a ring of yarn. The yarn may be tied at one or two places. If so, carefully untie these knots without disturbing the yarn ring.

2. Ideally, get a friend or willing relative to help at this point. He or she should hold the ring open with two hands. If you're on your own, put the ring over the back of an armless chair, or around two chairs if the skein is quite large. (If really desperate, use your knees.)

3. Find one end of the yarn and begin to wind around three of your fingers. After winding a few yards, you can pull this off your fingers and wind in the opposite direction, cinching the small ring you've made in the middle. Then just keep winding at different angles every few yards to create a solid ball. Don't wind the ball tightly, or you'll stretch out your yarn, which can wreak havoc on the size and elasticity of your crocheting. You're going for a ball with a comfortable squoosh, not a baseball.

Not every skein is perfect; you may have to stop from time to time to untangle the yarn before winding. It's also possible to buy a *swift*, a wood or metal contraption that holds the skein open and allows it to rotate for easier winding. Mechanical ball winders create perfect center-pull balls. These kinds of set ups can run $120 or so but can dramatically reduce the time you spend getting ready to knit or crochet. Most yarn shops or fiber supply catalogs feature at least one swift and ball winder combination. If you don't readily see one, just ask!

An important fact to note; different regions and stores label or refer to yarn differently. Whether it comes in a round ball, a log, or a twisted oblong, it's all just yarn.

Where Do I Find This Stuff, Anyway?

If you're already a knitter or a crocheter, you've probably gotten the knack for seeking out yarn in local (and not-so-local) yarn shops. But raw wool for wet felting and needle felting can be a trickier beast to track. Chapter 11 covers more hints and resources for finding the goods, but here are a few pieces of advice.

Your best bet is to look for a spinning and weaving supply store. Stores that sell primarily to hard-core fiber artists are likely to have the best selection of not only roving, both dyed and un-dyed, but felting needles, hand carders, and a variety of dyes. In the telephone directory pages, look for "Wool-retail," or even under "Art Supplies." If that doesn't work, call around a few of the local yarn shops. If the yarn shop doesn't sell roving or other felting supplies, most will know where their customers go to purchase these sorts of supplies. Art schools or colleges usually have a supply shop on campus, some of which are open to the public. Since many art programs have a fiber art component, these kinds of stores can carry basic supplies at reasonable prices.

Even more fun, take a road trip to your closest wool mill. Seeking one of these out can be a bit tougher. The Internet is a perfect resource as many felters before you have visited these meccas of fiber. Doing a search may pull up someone's blog that reviews one of her favorite shops. Visiting a wool mill or sheep farm sometimes lets you see a bunch of cute (and not-so-cute) sheep, alpacas, or llamas as well, which is always a bonus.

Yarns for felting are much easier to find. Look under "Yarn-retail," or sometimes "Wool-retail" in your telephone directory pages, or do a Web search for yarn shops in your town. When in a bind, some large craft stores carry one or two lines of shrinkable wool.

Finally, every supply required in this book can be purchased from many eCommerce shops online. What you lack in the tactile experience and instant gratification of shopping for fiber you can often make up for in convenience, selection, or price.

More shopping hints and tips can be found in chapter 11.

Getting Your Hands Wet

And now, it's time to start felting! The next three chapters cover the basics of wet felting, needle felting, and fulling. There's no particular advantage to reading them through in order. I do recommend reading a chapter through before attempting a project using that particular technique, unless you've had some prior experience.

Each chapter first covers the equipment you need to complete the sample projects. Then it teaches the basic principles through a series of quick-and-easy samples. These teeny, tiny projects are great for experimenting before you invest the time and cashola necessary for the fabulous projects in part two. Any more advanced techniques are then introduced, along with some troubleshooting Q&A and ideas for experimentation.

Once you feel comfortable with a technique, launch into some of the great projects in part two! Organized by type of project, these chapters give you a range of great items to challenge, inspire, and make your own through suggested variations.

Finally, part three covers back-up information. Are you a beginning knitter? Have you never crocheted? You'll find hints and tricks along with basic instructional info. Looking to expand your fiber stash? Chapter 11 covers shopping in detail. If you're a history buff, you'll love chapter 10's intro to the cultural history of felt. Any additional resources can be found in the appendix.

Hurry up—get felting!

Chapter Two

◆◆◆

Suds Party: Wet Felting

Take a little wool, a little water, and a little friction, and you can create unique and unusual fabric. Yes, it smells like wet sheep, but look how much fun you can have!

Wet Felting 101

The basic principles of wet felting are simple, as follows:

1. Put down a layer of wool with the fibers aligned in a single direction. The exact thickness of the layer can vary. Want thin felt? Try to make this layer as even and thin as possible. For thicker, more durable felt, you'll want to make each layer about a quarter of an inch thick. Don't worry about the thickness the first few times you try felting. You'll develop a more consistent technique for layering wool with practice.

2. Next, form a second layer, approximately the same thickness, with the fibers running at a 90-degree angle to the first.

3. Continue forming layers, making sure each layer is aligned perpendicular to the previous one. Most felt requires at least three layers.

4. Carefully apply a small amount of hot, soapy water . . . just enough to thoroughly saturate the wool without washing it out of alignment.

5. Press the water into the wool to make sure it's fully saturated.

6. Using your hands, a plastic bag, or other gentle tool, rub the wool very gently until it begins to adhere to itself. The rubbing can get more intense at this

point; continue until it seems safe to pick up the wool and flip it over. Similarly rub this side before flipping over again and repeating on the first side. Make sure to work the entire surface evenly.

7. After both sides are thoroughly matted together and a gentle pinch doesn't remove any fibers, the shrinkage begins. The felt is rolled up in a bamboo sushi mat, or other flexible yet textured item, and then rolled vigorously, first in one direction, then in another.

8. When the desired size and texture is obtained, the felt is washed, rinsed, and left to dry. It's that simple!

Tools of the Trade: What You Need to Get Started

In the most basic, primitive sense, wet felting only requires a few things: wool, water, and your hands or feet. Technically, this is enough to create felt the old-fashioned way. But, it's time consuming and often frustrating and can be made infinitely more fun and productive with a few modern conveniences.

The Fiber: Wool Roving

Although you can just as easily use alpaca, cashmere, angora, or llama, for the purposes of instruction (and in most of the projects) we'll use wool. Wool is cheap, easy to find, and felts nicely. Especially in the beginning, this is a very good thing. Unlike yarn crafts, where it's usually possible to simply unravel the project and start over, when wet felting, if something doesn't work out, you're better off starting over with fresh fiber.

When purchasing your first wool for felting, look for merino, Corriedale, or Blue Faced Leicester. Each of these varieties felts nicely. Although you can use natural-colored fiber, in the beginning it's fun to work with pre-dyed fiber. Color's never a bad thing! Most fiber supply stores stock a small selection of dyed wool roving. To economize, you can always use the dyed roving only on the

Wool roving.

top few layers, with un-dyed roving in the middle. If planning on working this way, make sure to match your fiber types. Using merino for the outside layers and Corriedale for the inside may cause problems due to the different speeds each fiber felts. For now, start with 8 ounces of a single type of fiber, either dyed or un-dyed. This will be plenty for the several small mini-projects in this chapter, including lots of room for error.

The Water Works: Tea Kettle, Tea Towel, Water, and Soap

As you've already read, using hot water helps open up the scales on the individual fibers, which in turn, allows them to more quickly interlock and mat together. Unless you're blessed with a built-in boiling water tap, you'll need a tea kettle or large stockpot to heat your water to

boiling. Planning on felting away from the stove? A cheap electric kettle can get you hot water very quickly, with any outlet. My electric kettle cost less than $20, and heats water to boiling in less than 5 minutes; much quicker than just using the stove.

Tea kettle, liquid measuring cup, and dish soap.

A little bit of laundry detergent or dish soap is also essential. The suds will provide a layer of protection to the fibers that allows for a tiny bit of friction without overly disturbing the layers. Soap also speeds up the felting process by opening up the fibers even more

How NOT to Boil Water

It may sound silly, but there is a right and wrong way to boil water. The wrong way involves your microwave. Even if you do this all the time, bringing water to a boil in the microwave is extremely dangerous. During the process, the water is heated to a much higher temperature than a stovetop boil. When using a stove to boil, any higher temperature points are brought to the surface with tiny bubbles that explode into the air and release steam. When a microwave heats water, the steam isn't released as it heats. Instead, a relatively calm-looking container of "boiling" water can be removed from the microwave. It's then a bit of a shock and surprise when something's added, and the surface seems to explode, sending scalding water cascading over the side of the container. This happens more frequently when a very clean mug or Pyrex container is used, or when reheating water that's still hot from the last boil.

While some microwaves now contain a beverage setting that can reduce the risk, it's still best to heat the water the right way; on your stove top.

The right way involves using a tea kettle or soup pot filled 2/3 of the way with tap water, and a stove top. Set your burner to high and wait for the pot to come to a rolling boil. Depending on the depth and quantity of water, it can take 10-20 minutes to come to a boil. At this point, the surface will be bubbling and steam will be rising heavily. Yes, the pot will boil even if you look at it. Take the pot or kettle off the burner and turn the burner off. For the best felting, use the water as hot as possible without risking burns.

If you're working in the backyard, basement, or garage, you can safely heat water using an electric tea kettle. These babies are available almost everywhere for around $20.

than water alone. Every felter has a soap preference. I've used either standard laundry detergent, in powdered form, or generic lemon-scented dish soap with equally pleasant results. Avoid detergents, such as Woolite, that are designed to be gentle. You actually want the harsher soap action to help open up those fibers.

I like pouring a bit of the hot water into a glass measuring cup before mixing in the soap. This lets the water cool slightly before beginning to work. You'll need clean water for rinsing and washing the felt when finished. Either keep a tub of clean water on hand or felt near the sink or bathtub.

Why have a tea towel? You can set it on top of your wool before wetting to make sure any delicate color work doesn't distort or float away. Since dyed fiber may bleed, and since hot water can damage delicate cloth, you obviously don't want to use an heirloom towel for felting. A sheet of nylon mosquito mesh works fine too.

A Little Damage Control: Plastic Gloves, Towels, Felting Container

Since you'll be working with hot, soapy water, you'll probably want to take some steps to protect yourself. Thick plastic gloves can help your fingers manipulate the wool without subjecting sensitive hands to the damp, hot wool. Having a few towels on hand can keep any spills under control. You'll also want a container for felting in, unless you're working outside with exceptionally large pieces of felt. The container should have sides that are tall enough to hold any excess water. It should also be at least a few inches larger on all sides than the layers of wool you start with. I like to use a plastic dish draining tray set up by the side of my kitchen sink. This lets the excess water easily drain off the one side, keeping my wool sudsy without danger of drowning. You can

Gloves, tea towel, and plastic dish draining tray.

also work effectively in a shallow casserole dish or baking tray. For larger, or longer, pieces of felt, you'll probably be working in a garage, basement, or backyard. In this case, I'll simply layer large plastic garbage bags on the floor, deck, or table, and felt on top of this.

Pulp Friction: Bamboo Rollers, Plastic Bags, Bubble Wrap

I'm a huge fan of the plastic bag. Wadded up garbage or thin shopping bags make great frictioners against wool when it's in a fragile, barely felted state. Clear plastic baggies can be placed over gloved hands so you can see what you're doing while not overly agitating the wool. Bags can also be used as a protective layer over complicated designs for the very first stages of felting. I'll cover this approach in the directions later in the chapter. Sheets of bubble wrap are also handy. Place them on top of your working surface, bubble side down, to add gentle friction to the underside of your project.

During the final stages of felting, you'll need some sort of heavy friction. Although some texts suggest corrugated tin washboards, they can be a little difficult to find these days. I like bamboo mats that are ordinarily used for rolling sushi. Usually available even in your grocery store for a buck or less, they're perfect for small pieces of felt. For anything larger than the mat, you can use inexpensive bamboo window shades. IKEA, dollar stores, or local discount house wares shops are great sources for these.

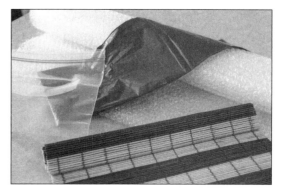

Bamboo mats, blinds, and plastic bags.

Other Handy Supplies

Don't limit your creativity to my suggested felting kit! Some felters swear by the ridged plastic lids to old Tupperware containers. Others wouldn't be caught dead without mosquito netting to be used as a porous protective layer during the wetting phase. (I use a tea towel or clear plastic bags.)

Felting Studio in a Box

It's a nice luxury to be able to set aside a full day for wet felting. The time it takes to assemble your equipment and set up a working area can eat into the time you actually spend creating. For the time-crunched, you can save a lot of time and hassle by setting up a felting studio in a box. This way, all your materials are on hand and well organized so you can spend more time felting and less time hunting and gathering.

What you need:

- Plastic tote box with a lid. Look for one that's at least 2 ft. long and 8 in. deep. Under-bed storage boxes work well, both from a size and storage perspective.
- Basic supplies mentioned in this chapter. At minimum, gather your raw fiber, felting notebook, pen or pencil, plastic bags, clean kitchen towels, measuring tape, bamboo mat or bubble wrap, and glass liquid measuring cup. The tea kettle, you can always steal from the kitchen when you need it. Chances are, you'll be working in the kitchen anyway. Consider keeping this book near your kit as well. It's a great reference and perfect for quick felting project ideas.

By keeping everything handy and in one place, you'll also be able to felt on the go. Just take the box over to a friend's house and throw a felting party!

For *resist felting*, a technique where you felt a three dimensional object around a template, sheets of heavy vinyl or plastic can be purchased at most fabric stores. (Read more about resist felting later in this chapter.) If you're planning on working with wool batts, a drum carder or set of hand carders will allow you to properly align the fiber before layering. Having some thick paper on hand for a template when laying out your layers comes in handy when creating specific shapes. Finally, you'll be surprised how often you'll look for a measuring tape (or ruler), a pair of scissors, and a notebook for keeping track of your experiments.

Setting up Your Work Area

Unless you're a full-time fiber artist (or blessed with a large trust fund), you'll probably have to set up a work area every time you want to felt. The area you choose will likely depend on your housing situation as well as the project you want to make. For smaller projects, I like to work on my kitchen counter, next to the sink. This position lets me set up my draining tray as my wet working area, while staying close to the stove for heating water and the fresh water tap for rinsing my work.

Before beginning any project, gather all your materials, even the ones you aren't sure you'll need. You're less likely to create a huge drippy mess if you don't have to run all over the house looking for stuff with wet hands and clothes. Even your outfit matters. For example, you probably don't want to felt in bare feet. Wear thick socks and shoes to keep your toes protected from dripping hot water. For the same reason, consider long pants. Since you'll be wearing tall plastic gloves, sleeves are less important. In fact, I usually choose tees or tanks to avoid dipping longer sleeves in my project, potentially messing it up. A work apron can help protect your clothes from getting overly messy. Don't forget the clean towels! Even if you have an easy-clean tile floor, you'll want to mop up any spills right away to prevent yourself (and your housemates) from slipping and falling on a forgotten puddle.

For larger projects, if it's nice out, I'll choose to work on my deck instead of in the kitchen. My electric tea kettle keeps the walking back and forth to a minimum. Instead of a felting tray, I like to layer large plastic garbage bags over the table, or the deck itself if I'm making something really large. Some felt artists will even work on the driveway when making yards of felt fabric. Basements work equally well for larger projects. A work table is handy, but you can work on the floor in a pinch.

Working with Roving

I know you're in a hurry to get started on some of the mini-projects in this chapter, but hang on for one more page or two while I fill you in on one more critical thing: In no type of felting is the handling of wool more important than in wet felting. For purposes of simplicity, and because I know you'd rather spend time felting than preparing wool, we're going to use wool roving throughout this book rather than unprocessed wool straight off the sheep. Roving has already been cleaned, carded and combed so that all the wool fibers face the same direction. It's also typically packaged in a user-friendly form that resembles a thick, slightly fluffy, length of rope. Most roving has been carded into a flatted tube approximately a half inch thick and two inches wide, and is most often sold by physical weight.

Fiber Properties

As briefly introduced in the previous chapter, different breeds of sheep produce fiber with different qualities. You'll hear serious fiber artists chat about the *crimp* of the fiber. This means the relative zig-zaggyness of the fiber. If you were to pull out one strand of wool, you'd see a texture ranging from relatively straight to quite curly. It's very similar to the differences in human hair, actually. For felting, a crimpier fiber will make a fuzzier felt. A smoother fiber typically makes a flatter and smoother felt. This book assumes that you want a finished project that's relatively smooth, flat, and sleek. For this reason, I recommend starting with merino, Corriedale, or Blue Faced Leicester for most of the wet-felting projects. Eight ounces of fiber will be plenty to complete all of the mini-projects in this chapter.

Another fiber property that matters is the physical length of each individual hair. This is called the *staple length,* and it will change the way you prepare the fiber for felting. While you don't need to determine the actual staple length of the wool you choose, it can be a fun experiment. Pull out a small fluff of fiber from your roving and gently separate with your fingers until you obtain a single strand of fiber. Straighten and measure. You'll probably determine a staple length of between 4 and 6 inches for most wools. Longer staple lengths just mean that you'll need fewer sections of fiber in each of your layers.

Preparing the Roving

If you're a spinner, some parts of this section will come as a bit of a review. The roving is typically a bit compressed and feels more like a solid, attached rope than it does bits of fluff. Roving can typically be anywhere from an inch to four inches thick. Think of the difference between a cotton ball and a cotton ball that's been played with by your cat until it resembles a big poofy mess. For felting, you'll want to create thin, even layers of fiber.

The easiest way to get this result is by spending a few minutes preparing your roving before beginning to felt.

The Split Stage

With *dry hands,* find one end of the roving and split into two sections, approximately the same thickness each. It's not important to split the entire hunk of roving, just enough to work with for the project you're about to start. With a little experience, you'll be able to fairly accurately estimate how much you'll need. In the beginning, prepare a little more than you think is necessary. It's always easiest to do this before your hands get wet.

The Fluffed Stage

Next, very gently pull apart the clump of fiber until it becomes very fluffy and evenly distributed. You should be able to hold it up to a light source at this time and see through it more or less evenly across. If any portions appear less transparent, use your fingers to even out the fiber.

The Wisp Stage

This step is probably best to do when you're ready to layer the fiber for felting. With your hands apart and very loosely holding the roving—think of cupping a small bird in your hands—gently pull your hands farther apart. As you pull, notice how the fibers slide against each other and out, rather than simply breaking. If nothing happens at first, slide your hands slightly further apart, and then farther apart until movement happens. Here's where staple length matters: your hands will need to be farther apart than the fibers are long.

You'll then have a relatively flat rectangle of wool, approximately the thickness of your fluffed roving and the length that corresponds to the fibers' staple length. In this image, the wisp is approximately 3 inches wide by 6 inches long.

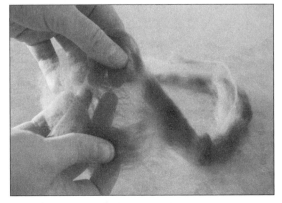

Fluffing the roving.

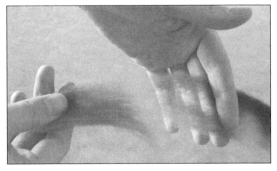

Pulling wisps.

Felted Snakes and Cords

The easiest wet-felting project, and the best place to start, is by making a simple length of rope. Consider it a cord, consider it a tube, consider it a snake toy for your kid or pet. However you think of it, this simple task has you rolling wool between your hands, with a little water, until it's firm.

What You Need

- Wool roving, prepared to the *fluffed stage* as directed previously
- Warm water in a bowl
- A small bit of dish soap or laundry detergent
- Spoon or stick for stirring

Roll Your Own

1. With your roving fluffed, as prepared previously, pull out a 6 to 8 inch wisp as directed for the *wisp stage*. Use your fingers to gently even out and align the fibers into an even length.

2. Add a small bit of soap to the bowl of warm water and stir to mix. You don't want the water to be scalding hot at this point. In fact, warm tap water works just fine. The friction of your hands will be enough heat for this project.

3. Dip your hands in the water to moisten. Sandwich the end of the length of fiber with your two hands and gently roll while applying a small amount of pressure. If making a long rope, keep the other end from fluttering around and disintegrating by weighing it to the work surface with a book or bar of soap. Start rolling very gently. If you get too frisky with the wool, it may break apart rather than form the nice smooth rope you're looking for. Continue to roll your hands around the rope, working from one end to the other, gradually applying more pressure.

4. It should only take a few minutes to make a rope. As you roll with your hands, the wool will become more stiff and dense. Make sure your hands stay wet during the process. Without water, the wool will not felt. In the same way, make sure your hands aren't too wet. The wool shouldn't become so wet that it easily breaks apart into a soggy mess. That's bad.

To dry, you have a few options. If you have one of those contraptions designed for air drying washed sweaters, you can place your felt on top of it and wait until it drys. Alternatively, for some projects, you can pin to a clothes line, or hang in your shower until dry.

When finished, the rope will look exactly like a skinny, solid tube of felt. Surprise! You can get creative by making multi-colored ropes, thin ropes, thick ropes, or even ropes with a dry, unfelted end for attaching to flat felt.

Gently align fibers into an even length.

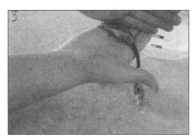

Roll rope gently in your hands.

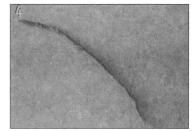

Finished felted rope.

At first glance, felted ropes may not seem all that glamorous or useful. But by leaving at least one end of the rope dry, fluffy, and unfelted, you can incorporate a rope into a piece of flat felting to make button loops, straps, or edgings. For an example of a dry-ended rope used with flat felt, see the Moleskine Book Jacket in chapter 8. You can also make a rope by felting around a thin object, such as a length of wire or pipe cleaner.

Balls and Beads

Not much tougher than rope felting, making felted beads and balls is another easy and quick project that can be applied to jewelry or even used as embellishments. You can even felt a ball around a ball-shaped cat toy, perhaps stuffed with catnip?

What You Need

- Wool roving, prepared to the *fluffed stage* as directed previously
- Warm water in a bowl
- A small bit of dish soap or laundry detergent
- Spoon or stick for stirring

Roll that Ball

1. With your roving fluffed, as prepared previously, pull out several 6 to 8 in. wisps as directed in the *wisp stage*. Usew your fingers to gently even out and align the fibers into an even length. Start by folding one wisp in quarters to make a small ball, similar to a cotton ball. Next, use portions of the remaining wisps and wrap around the outside of this cotton ball until you form a slightly compacted ball at least 2 inches in diameter. Remember, what you've formed so far will shrink dramatically when felted!
2. Next, add a small bit of soap to the bowl of warm water and stir to mix. You don't want the water to be scalding hot at this point. In fact, warm tap water works just fine. The friction of your hands will be enough heat for this project.
3. Dip your hands in the water to moisten. Sandwich the ball with two hands and gently roll while applying a small amount of pressure. Start rolling very gently. If you get too frisky with the wool, it may break apart rather than form the nice smooth ball you're looking for.
4. Continue to roll your hands in circles until the ball feels round and evenly felted.

If, at this point, the ball seems too soft, rinse it and let it dry. Dry felt is much more firm and solid than wet felt. If it's still too soft after drying, you can always felt it again.

| Make a ball. | Gently roll between your hands. | A finished felted ball. |

You can make solid colored beads, beads of different sizes, and beads that use multiple colors of wool in a marble effect. If you want to string your beads on a necklace, when still wet, use a sharp sewing needle to poke through from side to side. You may want to let the bead dry on a piece of string to keep the hole open enough.

You can also create beads from slightly felted rope. To do this, create a rope approximately the diameter of the beads you want. When it's still wet, cut or slice to make small tubes. Then, roll a slice between your hands into a sphere as with the roving ball discussed previously. You can also make other shapes as follows:

- To create a flat bead, make a large rope like a jelly roll and slice when dry.
- To create square beads, make a large bead and cut into a cube when dry.

See? The possibilities are vast!

A Roller Coaster: Your First Flat Felt

Hand-rolled felt has a lot of practical uses, but the age-old tradition of making flat sheets of felt, while more challenging, can be more satisfying. You can make purses, slippers, mittens, even blankets and yardage for sewing clothing. It uses the same principles of applying friction, heat, and water to fiber to get it stuck together and shrunk down into one cohesive object. But, instead of simply rolling the fiber around in your hands, you'll be creating several layers of fiber in a shape, then applying water, and finally friction to create a flat piece of felt. Since flat felt requires a little bit of patience and even more practice, we'll be making a small wool coaster as our first project.

What You Need

- Wool roving, prepared to the *fluffed stage* as directed previously.
- Water, heated to near boiling, now moved into a large liquid measuring cup. You'll need at least 3 cups for this exercise.

- Soap; I like liquid dish soap.
- Water-friendly work surface, such as a casserole dish, bathtub, or dish draining pan
- Heavy-duty plastic gloves
- Several plastic grocery bags or garbage bags
- Bamboo sushi mat for rolling
- Spoon or tool to mix water and soap
- Towels for clean-up
- Measuring tape or ruler
- Thin tea towel or nylon mosquito netting

Building Your Layers

1. Lay down ruler on work surface, and with fluffed roving, pull out a 4 to 6 inch wisp of roving as directed previously. Lay down roving on work surface above the ruler.

2. Complete the layer by placing similar wisps of roving next to and slightly overlapping the first until the desired size is obtained. For this project, you're looking for approximately 6 inches wide and 6 inches tall. Your first layer is now completed.

3. Build a second layer with the same size wisps as the first, but place each wisp perpendicular to the first layer. For example, if the first set of fiber was pointing left and right, this layer should be pointing up and down.

4. Continue to build layers of overlapping wisps, ensuring that each layer is positioned at a 90-degree layer to the previous one. Build seven such layers, trying to make each layer as even and consistent as possible in terms of thickness.

Lay roving above ruler.

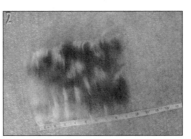
A completed first layer.

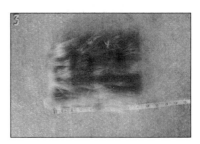
Laying new layer perpendicular to old layer.

5. When all the layers are built, you'll have a fluffy stack of fiber with ragged edges. Take this opportunity to gently push the edges of the fiber in to form more of a square shape. You'll also have the opportunity to adjust and straighten the edges of your felt during the felting process, but it helps to start off on the right foot. The height of your stack will vary based on your layering technique, and number of layers. Don't be put off by how tall it is! Once you add water, the stack will flatten to less than a half inch tall.

6. Now, add a little bit of the liquid soap or detergent to your pourable glass measuring cup of hot water. Use a spoon to mix in.

7. Next, very gently place the thin tea towel over the fluffy stack. This towel will help hold the wool in place while you wet it. Put on your heavy gloves before proceeding . . . you're about to work with hot water!

8. While pressing gently on the cloth, dribble on a bit of the hot soapy water. Gently press down with your hand, making sure the water fully saturates the stack of fiber. Repeat in different areas of the stack until the whole thing is wet.

Your felt should not be drowning at this point! If you find the wool is floating in a pool of water, gently tip the tray or dish to let some of the water drain. It should be thoroughly wet, like your hair after a shower, but not dripping like you're still *in* the shower. Also, if the wool is too hot at this point to touch comfortably through your heavy gloves, take a breather while it cools down slightly. You don't need to suffer for your art!

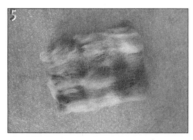

Push the edges in to make a square.

Cover with a tea towel.

Dribble some hot soapy water.

Place clear plastic wrap over the fiber.

9. Gently remove the tea towel, trying to disturb the fiber as little as possible. Place a layer of clear plastic wrap or a large clear plastic food storage bag over the felt. Press down on the plastic to remove any air bubbles and smooth out the wet wool.

10. With an extremely light touch, work your hands in a circular motion, beginning in one corner of the wool and moving steadily across the surface in small increments. This light friction is crucial. If you rub even a smidgen too hard, the fiber will shift out of its carefully formed layers and become a soggy, holey mess. If you find it tough to use such a light touch, do what I do; wad up a plastic shopping bag and gently rub this on the plastic instead.

Gently rub with wadded up plastic bag.

If you're working with clear layers of plastic, you'll begin to see the wool fibers sticking to each other and seeming more solid and uniform. The surface of the wool will also become covered with soap bubbles as you work. After several minutes, gently remove the plastic layer and use your bare fingers to check the progress by lightly touching the surface. If your finger doesn't cause any fibers to immediately shift, you're good to proceed.

11. Gently lift the felt and flip it to the other side. Replace the plastic layer and continue to gently rub this side with your fingers or a wadded plastic bag. You'll notice now that as you work, the wool will slide around on the work surface. This is a good sign! As this happens, you're actually creating a bit of friction on both sides of the wool.

Continue to rub the surface. As it becomes even more dense and uniform, you can rub with more pressure, or switch to using just your fingers. Make sure your hands are wet enough at this point; dry gloves or fingers can cause the wool to snag.

12. Periodically rotate the felt by 90 degrees, or flip it over, to make sure the felting is happening evenly across the entire piece. At this point, it's generally considered *soft felt*. The fabric is firm enough to generally bond together, but not so tight that it can't be felted further.

    This process can take from 5 to 25 minutes. Don't rush it; good, smooth felt takes time to create! My first six or seven attempts were miserable failures, mainly because I was in too much of a hurry.

When your felt seems fully solid and concrete, test it by pinching a bit of the fiber. If threads come loose immediately, you need to continue rubbing for a while.

Note: A common problem when beginning to felt is that your edges may be less solid than the center of the felt. If this is the case, just continue to work over the edges a bit more, using the same methods for applying friction. Don't hesitate to add more hot water and soap, if things feel a little dry.

If the whole piece of felt lifts off the surface, you're ready to move on. You've now created what's generally considered *hard felt*.

Rolling the Felt

13. Now, empty any excess water from your work area. Lift the felt and place your bamboo sushi mat down on the work surface. Place the felt on the mat and roll up, jelly-roll style.

14. Using your hands, vigorously roll the mat back and forth on the work surface. You're now adding a lot of friction to the mostly completed felt. This friction will quickly cause the felt to shrink in size as it becomes more dense.

Roll felt up in a bamboo mat.

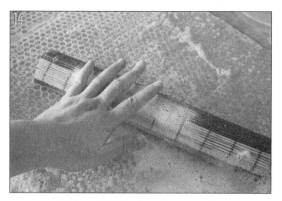

Roll mat back and forth vigorously.

15. After a minute or two, unroll the felt and reposition it on the mat in a different direction. Roll again. You'll want to repeat this repositioning process several times, since the portion that's at the center of the rolled up mat will be shrinking the most.

16. When it seems about as shrunken as it's going to get, you can gently rinse the felt in cool water to remove any excess soap. Squeeze out the remaining water, as much as possible, and let air dry. (For hints on drying, go back and read the last step in the felted rope directions earlier in the chapter.)

Blocking and Shaping

For the purposes of practicing, we don't much care what sort of shape we make, only that actual sturdy felt is created. But, let's say you're making pieces for a purse, or some other regularly shaped object. You'll want to shape the felt during the entire process: as you're laying out the fiber, as you're felting, and after you've rinsed the completed felt.

Shaping the Layers Using a Template

Forming square or rectangular shaped layers is relatively easy. You can lay out a ruler or measuring tape on your work surface and use this as a guide. But, if you're doing anything more complex, you may want to create a layering template. Even a piece of printer paper will work fine for this, although sturdier cardstock is probably a better bet. Follow these steps:

1. On the paper, draw out the shape you wish to felt, using a thick permanent marker.
2. Place the paper on the work surface and cover with a sheet of clear plastic wrap.
3. Layer the wool on top, being careful that all the fiber remains within the drawn line.
4. You can then felt as indicated previously, using the drawn design as guides.

This method is great for creating regular shapes such as triangles, rectangles, and circles, and any combination of them. However, since the resulting felt is going to shrink considerably, to have predictable finished measurements, you'll need to test the amount of shrinkage and size up your template accordingly.

Cutting Shapes from Soft Felt

1. When the felt is still in the soft felt stage, it's a great time to use a scissors to cut out more complex shapes. While you can free-cut the felt, you can also cut around a paper template. Just remember to cut the felt larger than your desired finished size. Since you'll continue to felt the object, it will continue to shrink. As with any felt, the exact amount of shrinkage can vary from fiber to fiber, and from technique to technique. Just know that felting is an inexact science. How much larger should you cut your shapes? Take a guess and see what happens. Or, follow the instructions later in the chapter for "swatching," or testing out, your felt.

2. After cutting the shape, use soapy water to continue to felt the object down to the hard felt stage as described previously.

3. Finish by rolling the object in a bamboo mat. You may not want to roll it too vigorously; you may distort your carefully planned shape!

Incidentally, after rolling and drying the felt, you can also trim it with a scissors into a particular shape. The edges will be much harder and crisper than if you were to do this when the felt is softer.

Wet Blocking

Just as knitters and crocheters know, wet wool is exceptionally pliable. After rinsing your felt, you can pull the edges into a particular shape, or stretch the felt around an object. For a great example of where wet blocking is not only effective but essential, see the Moleskine Book Jacket project in chapter 8.

Finishing Techniques

Depending on the type of wool you use, your felt may dry perfectly flat and soft, or more coarse and furry. If you like the look of a flat felt better, you can always press the felt with a hot iron. You can also use a safety razor to actually shave the surface of the felt. For more clean-up techniques, check out chapter 4's suggestions for finishing fulled objects. They apply equally well to wet-felted projects.

Felt on the Go

Many of the world's nomadic societies use felt as a practical, inexpensive, and incredibly durable fabric for everything from insulation to clothing. But, even the best felt does wear out over time. This worn-out wool, sometimes called *mother felt* can then be used to make a new, thicker piece of felt.

The *mother felt* is first laid on top of animal skins. Then, layers of sheep, camel, or goat fleece are built on top of the *mother felt*. Water is added to the whole thing, and then the assembly is rolled around a thick pole. The skins are then tied in place with rope so that no part of it comes loose to drag on the ground. Finally, and most amazingly, the pole inside the roll is attached to ropes that are in turn attached to the saddle of a camel or horse. As the animal walks, the wool rolls along behind it, gradually creating a thick piece of felt inside of the protective layers of skins.

Resist This!

Wet felting is good for more than just single sheets of flat felt. You can create pocketed or three-dimensional objects by using a sheet of heavy cardboard or plastic or a nonporous three-dimensional mold to felt around. In serious fiber art circles, this plastic mold is called a *resist* because it prevents the fibers from felting through it and attaching to each other.

In this mini-project, we'll use a sheet of cardboard or plastic to create a small, flat, seamless pouch.

What You Need

- All of the materials from "A Roller Coaster: Your First Flat Felt"
- A piece of heavy vinyl, plastic, or cardboard. If using cardboard, cover with packing tape or insert into an appropriately sized plastic food storage bag.
- Scissors

Preparing the Resist Template

1. First, decide what size you'd like the finished object to be. Remember, it's usually easier to start small since you won't be as tempted to rush. My first pouch-like purse was a mere 6 inches by 5 inches square after felting.

2. Cut the vinyl or cardboard to a square or rectangle approximately 10 percent larger than your desired finished size to allow for shrinkage. Also, since the "open" edge of the bag will end up shrinking slightly lower than the template edge, you may want to cut the template even a little longer to compensate.

3. Place the template onto the center of the work surface.

Building Layers and Applying Friction

4. Form the layers on top of the template, as described in "A Roller Coaster: Your First Flat Felt." Create six layers, making sure that the layers all extend at least an inch and a half further than three of the four template sides. The one that's layered even to the template will be the top of the bag. Use your fingers to push any stray fibers below the edge of this side of the template to form a neat, even edge. It's really important that the open side not stray over the template edge. Otherwise, it'll felt closed on all four sides, and you won't have much of a purse.

5. Place a tea towel over the wool and wet the portion directly over the template. Do not allow the edging of the wool—the part that extends beyond the template—to get too wet. Although it's pretty tough to completely avoid dampening the edges, by applying the soapy water to the very center of the wool and using your hands to gradually

dampen more and more, you'll have a little more control over the process. The important part is to avoid inadvertently felting these edges.

6. Following the instructions in "A Roller Coaster: Your First Flat Felt," begin applying gentle friction to the portion of the wool above the template. You want to avoid applying any friction to those edges.

7. As soon as the felt is stable enough, lift the wool with the template and turn it over so the template is on top. With dry hands, fold the first layer of the dry edge into the center of the bag. If the corners feel too thick, distribute some of the corner wool elsewhere. Fill in the empty center of the bag with more wisps of wool until you have six full layers on this side as well. When forming these layers, make sure to work in the edge layers by folding them in one at a time and matching their direction with the center wisps. It'll make sense when you do it . . . honest. Remember also to leave the same edge of the bag uncovering the template, as on the previous side.

8. After all layers are folded in and formed, work this side as for the first. (See step 5). Make sure to pay attention to the three "seam" edges. The folding of the edges will have partially secured them together, but you'll still need to apply friction especially to these parts. You can also add more fiber in as you felt to make a sturdier edge.

Make top even with template.

Apply gentle friction.

Fold first layer of dry edge into center.

Removing the Template

9. When the felt reaches the hard felt stage and using the pinch test lifts the bag rather than individual fibers, it's safe to remove the template. Because the wool might have slightly shrunk around the template, use care when sliding it out.

10. Now, wet and soap your hands and slide one into the pocket where the template used to be.

11. Rub on the inside of the pouch on both sides to fully felt the bag's interior.

12. After everything feels pretty stable, you can place one hand on the inside and the other on the outside of the bag and rub back and forth to continue to felt.

Finishing

13. Roll the bag in a bamboo mat to complete the shrinking process.

14. Rinse to remove any excess soap and squeeze to help dry.

15. While still wet, you can block the bag into a more square shape. To do this, cut your resist template down a little to be the appropriate size for the now shrunken bag. Place the template back inside the wet bag, and stretch the bag to fit.

16. Let dry with the template still inside.

Rub on the inside of the pouch on both sides.

You now have a handy little pouch-shaped bag. Sew on a cord for a strap, and you're set!

Just Try To Resist These Incredible Projects

For a more useful project that uses the resist technique, check out the Moleskine Book Jacket in chapter 8. You can also wet felt around a solid object. Most commonly, this will be a purchased mold that helps create hats, mittens, or slippers, but you can also felt around just about anything. Try wrapping the roving around a glass jar to create a wet-felted vase. Or, felt around an entire plastic index card box and then cut the top off to make a lid. Remove the box from the middle, and you'll now have a felt box. Wet felting three dimensionally around a form is possible but isn't for beginners. Because wet wool is slippery and tends to slip off the form quite easily, I'd recommend a few easier projects before attempting this advanced technique.

To purchase felting molds, do a quick search on the internet. Fiber arts shops, such as Marr Haven Farms (www.marrhaven.com) will often sell these molds and forms.

Nuno Felting

Also often called laminate felting, *nuno felting* is the art of felting wool to a gauze-like fabric, usually silk or cotton. As you've already seen, building a pure wool felt requires at least three layers for stability. By felting onto a pre-existing fabric, you can create thinner, more delicate felt that still has the strength of a much thicker piece.

Your fabric choice is really important for this technique. Because you need something the wool can stick to, and because wool doesn't typically felt onto slick fibers like cotton and silk, the fabric must be extremely porous. For best results, look for a fabric with visible holes throughout the weave.

In this mini-project, the technique we'll use is fairly different than the earlier flat felting projects. Like it this way better? Give it a shot for your other work as well.

What You Need

- Wool roving, prepared to the fluffed stage as directed previously. Use merino for the best results with finer fabrics.
- A 1.5 yd. (approx 4.5 ft.) length of silk or cotton chiffon. See previous notes for best fabric selection.
- Cold water. (Yes, I said *cold*.)
- Your preferred felting soap. I typically use liquid dish soap.
- Water-friendly work surface, such as a large table. You'll need as much room as your scarf is long.
- Swimming pool noodle.
- Heavy-duty plastic gloves.
- Length of bubble wrap or swimming pool insulation, at least as long as the chiffon.
- Bamboo window screen for rolling, at least as long as the chiffon.
- Sheer nylon mosquito netting to use as a wetting cloth. Make sure this is quite a bit longer and wider than the silk or cotton chiffon fabric. If felting on both sides of the cloth, you'll need netting that's twice as big.
- Spoon or tool to mix water and soap.
- Towels for clean-up.
- Measuring tape or ruler.
- Scissors or rotary cutter.

Why Do I Need a Noodle? What's the Cold Water for?

If you're reading closely, and I bet you are, you're probably wondering why you'd need a pool noodle. These heavy foam tubes can be purchased at home and garden stores or anywhere they sell pool supplies. The noodle comes in handy for felting large or long pieces because it allows you to felt by rolling from the start. By wrapping the layers of wool around the noodle and up into a jelly-roll of bubble wrap, felt, and noodle, you can apply gentle friction just by rolling.

Chances are, if you live in a seasonal climate, you won't be able to find pool noodles year-round. Instead, try any solid tube that's at least 4 inches in diameter. This could be some of that foam pipe insulation you can get at the hardware store. It could be a tall, plastic vase. Use your imagination and improvise, if you must!

As for the cold water, in this case, we don't want the wool to felt that quickly. It's essential that the wool have time to adhere to the fabric, too, instead of just sticking to itself. With hot water, often the wool will felt only to the wool layer and stay separate from the fabric.

Preparing the Fabric

Before beginning to felt, you'll want to cut the fabric into a scarf shape. A usual width is 6 to 8 inches across. Use a yard stick and rotary cutter for the most precision. Scissors work just fine, as long as you're careful.

Setting up Your Work Area for Large Felt Pieces

Because you're felting something quite long this time, you'll need more space. Although this can be done on the floor of your basement, garage, driveway, or deck, it's probably most comfortable if you have a table you can appropriate instead. Cover the table well with plastic bags or plastic sheeting to prevent water damage. You might also want to place sheeting on the floor underneath the table as well, to catch any excess water.

After preparing your table and floor, do the following:

1. Lay the bubble wrap or pool insulation on the surface, bubble side down.
2. Place the fabric in the middle of the bubble wrap and layer with wool, as you did earlier in the Flat Felt Making example. This time, since the fabric is porous and will adhere to the wool, you only need one layer. If you'd like some of the fabric to show through, concentrate on making your layer particularly thin in parts. This is a design process; you can do what you want with the scarf. Have fun, and experiment!
3. When complete, cover with the nylon netting to use as a wetting cloth.
4. Using cold water mixed with a little soap, gently wet the wool/fabric sandwich and press until saturated.
5. Decide whether you want the fabric to have felt on both sides or on only one side. If you're happy with one side, skip ahead to the next section. For a double-sided fabric, while wet and with the nylon still in place, carefully flip the entire scarf over so the fabric side is facing up. Repeat the wool layer on this side, add another nylon mesh layer, and wet this side as well.

The Easy Roll

Because rubbing, even gently, might disturb your few careful layers too much, to work nuno felt, you roll the assembly right from the start. So, do the following:

1. Place your pool noodle (or substitute) at one end of the scarf and roll up the entire thing, bubble wrap, nylon mesh, wool, and fabric, into a jelly roll.
2. With gentle even pressure, roll the "jelly roll" back and forth for about 5 minutes.
3. Carefully unroll and remove the nylon mesh before the wool adheres too much to it.

4. Re-roll and continue to roll back and forth for a further 15 to 35 minutes, checking occasionally on the progress. You'll notice the fabric begin to "pucker" as the wool fiber begins to felt. The wool will also begin to show through the reverse side of the fabric.

When the felt is secure and firmly adhered to the chiffon fabric, move on to the next step.

The Hard Roll and Finishing

Now, take the felt and roll it up in your bamboo window shade or blind. You can still wrap the scarf around the pool noodle to prevent the center of the roll from collapsing on itself and not felting as well as it should. Roll the whole thing back and forth vigorously, again checking the progress frequently. Using the bamboo for heavy friction should cause the scarf to continue to shrink in size at this point. As the wool shrinks, it will continue to pull the fabric in, and create gathers and puckers. After a few minutes, stop rolling, rinse the scarf, and lay flat to dry.

Tips and Tricks

You don't have to cover the entire piece of fabric to make nuno felt. Consider using the wool to make designs on the surface of the scarf instead. Also, use the tips in chapter 5 to pre-dye your fabric before felting. Using a contrasting color of wool will allow the color work to really show. For another example of what you can do with fabric and wool, check out Suzen Green's Scarf for the Subzero Urban Dweller in chapter 7.

Release Your Inner Artiste: Design for Wet Felting

Just like a knitter can choose different colors of yarn, making stripes or complex patterns with stitches, a wet felter can similarly play with color and texture in any project.

Color Play

In felting, you're only limited by the colors of wool you have on hand. Although it's usually possible to buy dyed fiber in your local shop, for the best flexibility and color range, you might want to consider dyeing your own wool. For hints and tips, check out chapter 5, where dyeing techniques are covered in detail.

So, let's say you have a palette of colored wool from which to choose. You can incorporate different colors or patterns of color in your project in a few different ways.

Using Hand-Dyed Wool

In addition to solid colors, wool roving can be found with multiple colors that create a variegated pattern. This wool has likely been dyed by hand, allowing several different colors to bleed and blend into the fiber. Using hand-dyed wool can be a quick and easy way to get some color into your fiber work. When you pull the wisps from a hand-dyed roving, each wisp will be unique. When the felting is completed, you'll end up with a marble effect. For an example, check out the Moleskine Jacket in chapter 8.

During the Layering Process

Combining different colors of wool while building layers is straightforward. What you see is what you get. You can make stripes, patches, or a reversible felt with a different color on the inside. You control the thickness and positioning of the fiber while building the layers. Keep a few things in mind, however.

First of all, the contrasting color must be aligned in the same direction as the other fibers of that layer; otherwise the felt might separate unattractively.

Secondly, you only really need to focus on adding the color to the outer one or two layers on the top and bottom. If you're working on a nine-layered stack, the middle five layers don't matter in terms of color. Provided you do everything right, those layers won't show. For this reason, many felters use undyed wool in the center of thick pieces, as it costs dramatically less than dyed fiber.

Finally, it's really important that the different colors shrink and mat at the same rate. For the best results, use the same breed of wool for the entire project.

Even so, it's probably a good idea to test out your combination by making a small 3 by 3 inch square, or something similar. This will also let you see whether any of the dye will bleed, or run, during felting.

This process, called *swatching,* is one of those best practices that no one wants to do, but that usually ensures better and more predictable results in the long run. Taking 10 minutes up front to swatch can save you from redoing the entire project later. For more hints on swatching, see the "Swatch It!" section later in this chapter.

Using Soft Felt Shapes for Inlays or Appliqués

To work more complex shapes, you can take two (or more) softly felted sheets in contrasting colors, cut them apart into various shapes, and then continue felting them together. See "Cutting Shapes from Soft Felt" earlier in this chapter. After your shapes are prepared, simply layer them on top of a base felt and continue felting as before. Some felt artists work this technique to make complex inlaid designs. Working with inlays can be tricky, since the soft felt edges need to line up precisely and felt as if one unified design. If this interests you, try it out on a small project first. Make two of the Roller Coaster mini-projects earlier in this chapter, and felt until the fibers are just beginning to adhere. Hold the pieces of felt together and cut a square out of the center of both. Then swap the middles and continue to felt so that you have two squares, each an inverse of the other. Pretty cool.

The trick with inlay felting using soft felt is ensuring that the inlays stick to each other. So, you really want to avoid over-felting initially. In the beginning, it's easiest to practice this technique by felting the pieces together on top of a third piece of soft felt.

Texture with Mixed Media

If you've worked through any of the mini-projects in this chapter, you've seen that layering is the key to building a piece of flat felt. However, you don't have to stick to wool! Just underneath the very top layer, consider placing designs of string, yarn, feathers, fabric, or other items. As long as the top layer can effectively sandwich your embellishments, they will be caught during the felting process as if inside quilted pockets. If your top layer isn't exceptionally thick, these embellishments will show through and give texture and design to your felt.

Shibori, a Japanese technique that involves stitching or folding fabric together before applying dye, produces a dye pattern that has incredible depth and interest. The areas that are sewn or bound together typically aren't exposed to the dye, and so are left in their natural colors. In recent years, fiber artists have been playing with the technique and applying it to add texture to flat felt. For an example that uses a modified Shibori technique, check out Shannon Okey's Octopillow in chapter 9.

Why not use this technique on your flat felt as well? Make sure the felt is at least at the soft felt stage before using string, twine, thread, or rubber bands to tie the felt together at places. Continue to felt by hand, or even use your washing machine set to hot, the same way you'd shrink a knitted item. (See chapter 4 for more information.) When the felt is fully felted, you should be able to remove the ties and have a nubbly, bumpy texture on the surface of your felt.

Final Thoughts and Inspiration

One of the most magical attributes of wet felting is the enormous potential the technique contains for creativity. More similar to sculpture or painting that many of the other fiber arts, wet felting allows you to create any form, any design, any structure. Wet felting simply begs for experimentation and innovation. Whether you simply have to get creative to find a more effective tool than the one you already have, or have a moment of wondering "What if I put this here?", you'll quickly find yourself enjoying the limitless potential of wet felting. As long as you can imagine it, you can probably find some way of doing it.

Troubleshooting

Wet felting is an art, or at least a fine craft. And, it definitely takes practice to make perfect. Don't be surprised if your first few experiments turn out as soggy disasters. Mine certainly did! Hopefully, these few hints will make your path a little smoother.

Swatch It!

Before making anything larger than a few inches across, consider felting a sample swatch. Keep everything as much the same as in the project as you can, except for the size: Use the same materials, build the same number of layers the same thickness as you intend to have for the final piece, and felt with the same attention. If any other techniques are included, such as adding a pre-felted cord, do this on the swatch as well. The idea is to test out all the variables before you invest a half pound of wool and half a day into making that gorgeous tote bag you've had in mind.

This is especially good advice when combining different colors of wool. Since different dye processes can affect the characteristics of the wool, the wools may felt at different speeds, even if they are the same breed. A little bit of swatching beforehand can suss out any problems before they become big problems.

When Combining Wools, Stick to the Same Breed

Just like you want to swatch when combining colors, it's especially important when combining different breeds of wool. For the best results, if your inner layers are merino, make sure that your outer layers are merino as well. While I've had success from time to time using different breeds together, the results can be unpredictable and spotty, at best. Especially when just starting to felt, make it easier on yourself. Do everything you can to get good results.

Be Patient

More than anything else, patience is essential with wet felting. It may be tempting to try to rush things along by rubbing a little more vigorously than suggested. But all that you'll accomplish is pushing the carefully arranged layers out of order, making lumpy bumps in some places, and wafer-thin swamp-moss in others. By keeping things gentle as long as possible, you'll end up with a smoother, more even felt. You'll end up with something you can use and enjoy.

How do you know what pressure to use, when to apply more? There's no hard rule, but your fingers are a good guide. As long as the fibers feel slightly loose and slidey under your hands, you want to keep the pressure as light as possible; so light that you're barely touching the surface. It might feel like you're not accomplishing anything, but do this for a few minutes, and you'll soon see that the surface of the wool is becoming felt-like. As the fibers begin to feel more solid and move less, and the entire stack slides around a little with each touch, you're safe to add more pressure.

Keep It Wet

When the wool and your hands begin to dry out, the fibers will stick to the pads of your fingers and will tear off. This is the opposite of what you want to do! Don't be afraid to add a little more soapy hot water if you feel you need to. You can always pour off excess water, but after the felt dries and disintegrates, it's tough to correct. Keep in touch with what you're doing. The wool should feel like a damp, smooth sponge. It should also quickly build up a layer of soap bubbles. If the wool is merely wet and doesn't create suds within a minute, add a bit more soap. Soap is a very good thing with felting; don't hesitate to add more if you feel you need it.

Try, Try, Try Again

You heard this one all through grade school, didn't you? If at first, you don't succeed . . . don't give up. Wet felting takes a lot of patience and a lot of practice. You may breeze through the sample projects but run into some difficulties in the project chapters. Maybe your felt is too thin in places and easily breaks apart. Maybe your decorative layers slide off during the final rolling stage. Maybe the whole thing just slides off the resist and looks like a damp puddle of seaweed. You can sometimes fix these kinds of problems. Holes can be patched using needle felting. Decorative layers can be attached, again, with needle felting. See the next chapter for the details on these handy tricks. But, if the felt just refuses to work, it's better to just start over, to take it more slowly the next time, and to pay more attention to what you're doing.

It's really easy to get complacent, to assume that because it worked x number of times, it'll work just as easily the next thousand projects, too. But, every project is different. Larger pieces of felt, for example, can be harder to effectively complete. Using different types of wool can also affect how quickly or slowly you have to work.

When all else fails, don't give up. Take a breather from felting for a day or so. Go out and buy some fabulously dyed merino to inspire. Take a step back and make something a little smaller next time. But know that you'll get it down, and as you have more experience, those little mistakes and failures will come further and further apart.

Chapter Three

❖

Poke, Poke, Poke: Needle Felting

With a special barbed needle, fiber can be appliqued onto fabric, other pieces of felt, or used to create three-dimensional felt without a single drop of water. Magic? Try it, and decide for yourself.

Why It Works

As you saw in the previous chapters, a single strand of wool fiber is covered in overlapping scales. With wet felting, the moisture, heat, and friction causes the scales to expand and open, allowing them to stick together. Needle felting uses the same general principle, but does away with the need for water and heat all together.

Instead, a barbed steel tool is used to repeatedly puncture the fiber. As the sharp needle moves through the wool, it attaches individual strands together; just like sewing without the thread.

In this chapter, we're going to look at a few different creative possibilities for needle felting: appliqués, three-dimensional forms, and needle felting seamless wearables.

Tools of the Trade: What You "Needle" to Get Started

Have you already tried creating flat felt with a wet-felting process? If so, you might feel overwhelmed by the amount of equipment necessary. Luckily, with needle felting, you need very little stuff.

Felting Needles

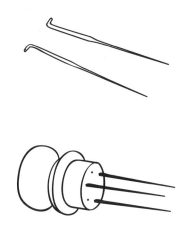

Approximately 3 inches long, these steel needles usually come in a diameter ranging from 32 to 42 gauge, similar to wire measurements. The higher the gauge number, the finer the needle and the more suitable for thinner fibers or smaller detailed areas. The lower the gauge, the thicker the needle and the better for use with coarse fibers. In the beginning, shoot for the middle of the road. I like working with 38-gauge felting needles for most purposes.

Each needle features an inch-long, very sharp tip that's studded here and there with tiny barbs. The non-sharp end of the needle is usually bent for easier holding. Since the sharper the better, needles should be replaced when they start to feel dull. Luckily, these babies will set you back only a buck or so per needle. For a little more, you can purchase a holder that lets you use three or more needles at one time. The one pictured here holds up to six, which can be a time-saver for larger areas of felting.

Polyurethane Foam

To protect your felting surface (and yourself) and prevent needle breakage, a 2-inch thick sheet of polyurethane foam is essential. This foam should be placed underneath the fabric you'll felt on. For felting on one side of a pocket, such as a bag, foam can be cut and inserted to prevent the needle from stabbing through both layers of fabric. As you'll also see later in this chapter, foam is handy to cut into shapes for seamless 3D felting.

Clover, a notions manufacturer and distributor, makes plastic brush-type bases that are great for small needle felting projects. The drawbacks? They can be tough to find, and aren't always available in your local supply store. Also, you lose a lot of the flexibility that the much cheaper foam provides. While you can cut the foam to different sizes, depending on the size of your project, the plastic brush bases are only available in set sizes up to 5.5 by 3.5 inches.

Fiber

For needle felting, any kind of un-spun wool is fantastic. Stick with pure wool, or blends of wool and other fibers. Try out a wool/silk blend to add a little bit of sheen to your project. It's fun to use bits of yarn for outlines and fine detailed work, too. As with the fiber, make sure the yarn has a significant animal-sourced content. Look for pure, non-Superwash wool, or wool/mohair blends for the easiest felting. However, go ahead and experiment! Many other yarns, as long as they're sticky enough, will needle felt nicely with a little extra care.

Something to Felt on

For appliquéd needle felting, you'll need something to felt on. It's probably most common to needle felt on top of other wool felt; either created through wet felting or by fulling a knit or crocheted fabric. But, don't let this stop you! You can also needle felt on top of many commercially woven fabrics. See the Bad Boy Hoodie in chapter 7 for a great guy-friendly example.

Other Handy Supplies

As mentioned earlier, it's nice to have scissors, pens, notebook, and measuring tapes or rulers available when you work on any felting project. For detailed appliqués, many drawing-challenged felters prefer to have handy a set of stencils in some cool designs. You can use these stencils for initially placing the fiber, or as a template during the felting process, if the design is large enough. When using stencils, be aware that the tougher stencil plastic can break the tips of your needles. Exercise a bit of care, and you'll save on frustration later.

Machine Needle Felting

While it's probably easiest (and definitely cheapest) to start with a few hand-held needles, many crafters–especially quilters–opt to purchase a *needle felting attachment* to be added to their sewing machines. By mechanizing the process, it's possible to needle felt large designs on top of fabric with very little manual effort.

Monogramtastic: Playing with Needles

Here's a chance to see just how easy needle felting appliqués can be.

What You Need

- Wool roving, small pieces in various colors
- 10 or 15 yards of wool or wool-blend yarn for detail work
- Felting needle, at least one
- Small foam pad, at least 2 inches thick, approximately the size of the area you wish to needle felt upon
- Scissors
- Flat wool felt or fabric. This is a great chance to use the flat felt sample from chapter 2!

Design Away

First, decide what kind of design you'd like to do. My first needle felting project was a big, bold letter A. Pull out fluffy bits of the wool and use your fingers to arrange on top of the fabric so it looks like the shape you'd like to make. You can continue to adjust as you needle felt, so there's no need to make it perfect at the beginning.

Unlike wet felting, it's not essential to align the fibers in any particular direction. Just push and prod them into the desired shape and start at it.

Poke, Poke, Poke

Holding the needle in your dominant hand, stab directly in and out of the fiber. At first, the fiber will pucker down and shift, so make constant adjustments to keep your design in the right shape. Evenly move along the design, plunging the needle in and out of the fiber, fabric, and foam beneath. Be careful to not pull the needle out on a different angle than it went in. The extra pressure could easily cause the needle to snap. Also be conscious to keep fingers, arms, and other fleshy parts out of the way. These needles are sharp!

After several minutes of work, the loose wool should start to resemble a piece of felt. Continue poking the needle through the fiber until it's impossible to shift any fibers with your fingers. From time to time, lift the fabric and fiber off of the foam base to make sure you're not permanently sticking it to the foam.

Drawing Outlines

You can now use the yarn to draw outlines around the design. Lay the yarn in place around the monogram. Again, use the needle to stab the yarn repeatedly, until it's unlikely to shift position.

Finishing Up

Once the fiber has been thoroughly felted to the fabric, you should see bits of it sticking through the reverse side of the fabric. This really means that it's been well attached. Of course, depending on how thick the fabric is, you may see only a little bit, or none at all. On a garment-thin piece of fabric, you should expect to see quite a bit of the fiber on the reverse side.

If you're looking for a smoother felted appearance, you can now apply a bit of warm soapy water, and rub with your hands in a circular motion. Yes, this is wet felting, but sometimes it can change the finished look of needle felted appliqués. Some needle felters will also put the piece in the washing machine for a cycle to further bond the fibers together. One note of caution; this should only be attempted with pure feltable fibers. Machine washing a blend of silk and wool may have less than stellar results. As before, I highly suggest testing any risky technique out with a swatch first.

Some needle felters prefer to take a pet brush or comb to the work after finished. Combing the surface will fluff out the fiber and make a more furry appearance. As with the wet finishing, the final choice is up to you.

Troubleshooting: When Good Felt Goes Bad

Thankfully, needle felting isn't that complex of a concept. Not that many truly bad things can happen when needle felting. Here are some tips that helped me while I was learning.

You CAN Turn Back Time

With needle felting, you can almost always undo something that didn't work out, especially if you realize the bad news before the appliqué is completely attached. Just pull off the appliqué or offending piece if working in three dimensions. Many times, you can then use your fingers to refluff the wool so it's ready to be used again. If the surface of the needle felt you wish to keep now looks puckered, just a little rubbing or wet felting can make it look good as new. (Let it dry, however, before needle felting on it again—see the following section.)

Broken Needles Can Be Heart Breaking

Does your needle keep snapping? Be careful to stick the needle directly in and out of the fiber without twisting it or turning it while in the *in* position. You always want to bring it out the same way you put it in. Even a little bit of rotation can break the needle tip.

Do not, under any circumstances, be tempted to needle felt on something wet! The moisture in the fibers will make them too tough, and your needle will likely break. Wait until the piece has fully and thoroughly dried to save yourself some headaches.

Finally, make sure to amply cushion the piece while needle felting. Plunge too deep, and you might go through a thin piece of foam and hit the table beneath. Use controlled pokes, and you'll have greater success.

Safety First

This one bears repeating. Felting needles are designed to be incredibly, if deceptively, sharp. It doesn't take much pressure to break skin with the sharp point of a new needle. Keep your hands and fingers clear of the needle and work slowly enough so you have full control of where you poke the needle every time. Getting tired? Put the project down until your patience returns. Rushing things only causes you to rush to the medicine cabinet for bandages.

Avoid unexpected stabbing by using the same care when storing your supplies. Felting needles are often sold with the sharp end protected by coffee stirrers or skinny drinking straws. Always replace these guards before putting your needles away. The last thing you want is to stab yourself when starting a new project. If using a needle holder for multiple needles, it's probably best to cover the needles in the holder and put the whole thing away. If this isn't possible, remove the needles first, then cover, then store.

Practice Makes Perfect

Remember, needle felting, although straightforward, still takes some practice to get the technique down. In the beginning, use scrap wool to practice on pieces of scrap fabric. You'll feel more free to experiment—and make mistakes—than if working on an heirloom-quality project where the stakes are much, much higher.

Endless Poking Possibilities

Even though appliqués are the most common use for needle felting, don't let this limit your imagination. With a little inspiration, you can needle felt three-dimensional objects such as dolls, jewelry, and flowers. Check out chapter 8's Spring Is Sprung! for a good starter project in three-dimensional needle felt.

You can also felt around a foam form to make seamless items like mittens, pouches, and hats. The foam shouldn't be too thick, and you'll need to be careful about the depth to which you plunge the needle. As with appliqué needle felting, you'll want to pull the fiber off of the foam from time to time to keep it from getting permanently stuck.

One of my favorite newfound uses for needle felting is for making small repairs to other felt. For example, let's say you have spent hours wet felting a purse, only to discover a small hole. Once the piece is dry, add fiber to the area just like a patch, and needle felt in place.

Need inspiration? Check online. Searching for "needle felting" brings up photos of finished pieces, instructions, and more. Subscribing to a general fiber arts magazine, such as *Fiber Arts* or *Selvedge* (see chapter 11), can also be a great source of ideas to enhance your practice.

Chapter Four

◆◆◆

Totally Full of It

Are you a knitter or a crocheter? Do you weave like a maniac? Creating a felt fabric out of a previously knitted, crocheted, or woven fabric is addictively fun. Plus, you get to use your washing machine for something other than laundry! What could be better than the perfect excuse to procrastinate from doing housework?

What's Fulling? What's Felting?

As I've mentioned earlier in this book, chances are—if you're a dyed-in-the-wool knitter—that you've heard the process of knitting something out of wool and shrinking it in the washing machine described as *felting*. But, speaking strictly technically, that process is actually *fulling*. So, that cute felted bag pattern in the latest magazine is technically a *fulled* bag.

Am I just full of it? You can decide that on your own. The core difference between felting and fulling is pretty simple. *Felting* creates a non-woven sheet of matted fiber by applying heat, moisture, and friction. *Fulling* takes a woven or knitted length of fabric and applies heat, moisture, and friction to mat and shrink the fibers. Felting works from loose fiber. Fulling works from knitted, crocheted, or woven fabric. That's the only real difference.

Yeah, it's a bit confusing. Since this is a semi-technical book, it will use the proper terms. In your own craft, call it whatever you want. Just make sure to have fun.

What Happens and How It Works

Although the original art of fulling was typically completed by stirring a length of loom-woven fabric in a pot of boiling water until the fibers shrunk, modern-day fiber artists have a suitably modern approach. While you can full any fabric, including hand-woven ones, this book focuses on fulling from store-bought or handmade knitted or crocheted items.

Basically, what happens is this: You take a knitted or crocheted item and throw it in the washing machine with a little bit of detergent. Run the machine on a hot water cycle and wait. As the heat, water, and agitation of the washing machine works on the fabric, the stitches will shrink up and stick together. The overall size of the piece will decrease dramatically as well. Full the fabric long enough, and you'll be unable to see individual stitches at all.

After the piece has fulled completely, let it dry and then embellish as desired. Just as with needle felting, you have a final choice to make: the finishing of the surface. Take an animal brush to the surface, and you can create a furry and wild fabric. Or, use a disposable razor or scissors to tame the surface into a completely flat, completely smooth exterior. Anything goes!

Soft Fulling versus Hard Fulling

Just as you can create various textures by wet felting, you can produce a spectrum of fabrics and textures by fulling in the washing machine. If the knitted or crocheted pieces are still fairly flexible after fulling, and you can pick out individual stitches even though the surface has become fuzzy, it's considered *soft felt* and the process that made it, *soft fulling*. You may want to only softly full certain garments or blankets. A great example of the appeal of soft fulling can be seen in Belinda Fireman's Rainbow Bridge Baby Blanket pattern in chapter 9. For a fabric that you intend to drape, soft fulling is the way to go.

In contrast, you can continue fulling most yarns in the washing machine until they no longer resemble knitting or crochet in the slightest. In these cases, *hard felt* is created, and you can cut the fabric without worrying about its unraveling. Hard fulling is, therefore, ideal for anything that may require cutting or deconstructing after fulling. It's also perfect for sturdy items, such as bags. Chapter 6 is chock-full of fabulous bag patterns to explore.

Can soft or medium felt be cut without risk of unraveling? The short answer is "It depends." In general, fairly rough pure wools will hold together more securely no matter the level of fulling. When in doubt, test it out before you cut into your prize project.

Tools of the Trade: What You Need to Get Started

Have you ever accidentally shrunk a favorite store-bought sweater in the wash? If so, you've fulled (you'll learn more about why you might want to full a sweater on purpose later on in this chapter!). All you needed then or now is a washing machine, a wool sweater, one or two items to add friction, and a bit of detergent. Some of the fulling projects in this book will sound fairly similar and require no previous knitting or crochet experience. Just scour your local thrift store (or your own closet) for suitable shrink-worthy knitted garments and go at it.

Washing Machine

Whether you have an energy-efficient front-loader or an old school harvest gold top-loader, whether you wash in a Laundromat, your building's laundry room, or in your house, you can full. Since the idea is not only to heat and wash the wool but to abuse it as much as possible, the older your machine, the better. You just need to be able to set the water to hot and the water level to low. Ideally, you'll also be able to stop the machine mid-cycle. If you'll be felting in a front-loader, you'll find some tips in a sidebar later in this chapter. If you'll be using a coin-op machine, try to get one that can stop mid-cycle so you can periodically check the wool. If it can't, it's pretty likely you'll just need to bring a lot of change and prepare to sit through a few cycles. In this case, a lot of the same advice regarding front-loaders helps as well.

Of course, you can also full by hand. Yes, this is a labor-intensive process, not unlike what you've already learned about wet felting. The idea is the same as wet felting; rub the item against something with friction, adding hot, soapy water, and keep at it until it shrinks. That's about all we're going to say about manual fulling for the rest of this chapter. If you're determined, go read the advice in chapter 2 and try it out! Otherwise, beg or plead to borrow a friend's washing machine. It'll be worth it; honest.

Lingerie Bag (to Prevent Plumbing Problems)

During the fulling process, sometimes a fair quantity of wool will shed from the knitted or crocheted items. This can look as harmless as a single fluff ball, but over time, these clumps may cause your washing machine to clog, or even worse, your plumbing line to need a good auger. You can place a mesh wire filter on the inside of the drain tube from your washing machine, which can prevent problems from spreading through the rest of the pipes. These filters are available at most large hardware stores, where you can also find great information on how to install the filter, as well as what type of filter works best with your brand. As cool as you might feel doing the installation yourself, be aware that these types of filters will only prevent problems associated with your plumbing, and not with the machine itself.

Save a lot of heartache up front and buy a zippered lingerie bag. Made from small nylon mesh, these bags will allow most of the fuzz to be trapped inside and are still porous enough to allow thorough fulling. Although not quite as secure, an old zippered pillowcase can do the trick. Standard pillowcases can also be securely knotted in place.

Old Sheets (for Friction)

You can just stick the item (in its bag) inside the washing machine and let the hot water do the work, but for quicker felting, add a few items to further abuse the project. Some books and online instructions suggest towels. Resist that temptation! Towels are made of cotton terrycloth that sheds lint during the wash. That lint is more than likely to be sucked up into your fulling project, which will soon be covered with nonremovable fluff, exactly the color of your towels.

Instead, I like old, smooth cotton pillowcases or twin-sized sheets. You don't need very many. . . two or three pillow cases or one twin flat sheet is enough agitation in most cases.

You can also try a tennis ball, an old pair of tennis shoes, or jeans that are now too old or small to be wearable. (If you've washed the jeans enough, they shouldn't run.) However, these items can potentially be too hard on your machine, so should be used only in machines old and sturdy enough.

Soap on a Rope (Just Kidding)

You don't need to worry about any kind of fancy soap or detergent for fulling. Although you usually want to keep your whites bright and your darks darker, for fulling, any kind of standard detergent is just fine. Whatever you use for laundry day will work wonderfully.

Mad Yarn Skillz

The fun really begins when you take a little needlework knowledge and craft the fabric before you shrink it. So, brush up on your knitting and crochet. Feeling a little rusty? Chapters 12 and 13 of this book give you some basic how-to in both crochet and knitting. Anything more complex, or specific to the pattern, will also be explained in the project instructions.

Haven't knitted or crocheted before? Although you can teach yourself from the info in chapters 12 and 13, it's probably better to invest in a course or book more focused on these basic skills. Check out *Not Your Mama's Knitting* and *Not Your Mama's Crochet* for more help.

To complete the fulled projects in this book, you'll need to be fairly confident with the following skills:

- ◆ Knitting You should know how to cast on, knit, purl, cast off, and execute work increases and decreases. Some projects are knitted in rows and others in the round. For some projects, such as Dana Codding's Don't Give the Mittens, you'll also need to be adventurous enough to try multicolor knitting. Intimidated? Don't be! Since fulling involves shrinking stitches until you no longer see 'em, most mistakes will simply be washed away. Learning new knit skills on a project destined for the washing machine can be a great stress-free way of trying something new.

- ◆ Crochet Hook-loving fullers should know the basic stitches in crochet: chain, slip stitch, single crochet, and double crochet. Experience working in the round as well as back and forth in rows is also handy. But, just as knitted projects are forgiving when fulled, crochet also hides many common stitch errors.

- ◆ Needles & Hooks Of course, since you'll be knitting or crocheting, you'll need the appropriate needles and hooks. Fulling happens more evenly and quickly if the item is knitted or crocheted quite loosely. So, don't be surprised if your pattern suggests a hook or needles several sizes larger than what you'd normally use with that thickness of yarn. A good general rule of thumb is to go up 50 percent of the original needle size.

So, if you'd typically knit on a US 6/4.0mm needle, as for a worsted-weight yarn, you'd want to knit the item on a US 10/6.0mm needle for fulling.

But, you don't have to worry intensely about the needle or hook selection. The pattern will give you an idea of where to start. As with any other project, you should check your gauge before beginning. Later in this chapter, you'll find more information on gauge for fulling.

Swatch Up Front

Yes, it takes a little time, and it delays a bit of the excitement of starting a brand new project. However, taking a few minutes to make a swatch (in other words, knit or crochet a 4 × 4 test square) and then run it through the machine to test the fulled results not only saves time in the long run, but money as well. In the past, I've skipped this vital step while designing bags. And, I have a stack of failed fulled bags in my closet—a waste of hundreds of dollars of yarn that could have been prevented with a little swatching. One yarn was gorgeous in the skein, but much too loosely spun to felt evenly. It looked like a wad of pink mashed potatoes when it came

The Language of Yarn

If you've just started knitting or crocheting, or haven't yet begun, some of the terms thrown around when talking about yarn may make your head all spinny. When in doubt, ask! Here are some of the terms you absolutely need to know.

Gauge and **Weight** are similar concepts. The gauge of a yarn is the number of stitches and rows you get to a 4 × 4 inch square. The ball band of the yarn will give you a recommended gauge, which usually only applies to knitted fabric, such as what you'd find in a sweater. The more generic weight of a yarn is a way of discussing a range of yarns that knit or crochet to similar gauges. For example, worsted weight yarn can be easily knit at 19–21 stitches to 4 inches. Bulky weight yarn is more like 8–9 stitches to 4 inches.

Ply describes the number of spun strands that are twisted to make a single piece of yarn. Yarns are most commonly found in single to 4 ply, but it's possible to find 6-, 8-, or 12-ply yarns as well.

Schematic diagrams show specific dimensions of a finished product. For fulling, these dimensions may reflect the pre-fulling size or the post-fulling size. In either case, the diagram will be clearly marked as such. For fulling, the finished size is usually approximate.

Swatching is the process of knitting or crocheting a sample before committing to the project. It's a great way to check the gauge for any piece, but for fulling projects, it's also ideal for determining the shrinkage of the yarn as well as the resulting fabric.

For more information on yarn for fulling, see chapter 1.

out of the wash. Another hand-dyed thick and thin yarn refused to full and simply got hard and lumpy. Both yarns were beautiful and could have been saved for some other project in the future.

The Problem of White Yarn

It's never more important to swatch than when using white or off-white yarn. Because many white or cream yarns have been bleached, they may be entirely resistant to shrinkage.

So, how do you know which whites will have a chance of working? The brand suggested in a pattern that uses white or off white should be a safe bet. Just make sure to use the exact same color. For example, an off-white may be fine while the pure white from the same brand won't work. Any pure wool labeled as organic should also be fine, as it should not have been subjected to any chemicals during processing. Finally, your local yarn shop may have some helpful information on hand. In any case, do continue to swatch even if you think the yarn will be fine. Changes or variations in the manufacturing process can make your skein refuse to cooperate.

Experiment with Blends

Yet another good reason to swatch, experimenting with blends of yarn can also yield different but fun results. For example, try fulling a wool/silk blend. Try holding a strand of novelty yarn together with a pure wool. Or, work with a bouclé mohair with a nylon binder. In all these cases, the wool or mohair will shrink while the other fibers won't. This can result in some very cool, very fashionable results. In addition to getting the chance to approve the final fabric, swatching also lets you compare shrinkage. Since blended yarns may shrink less overall than a pure wool, being able to check the finished size ahead of time can prepare you for unexpected results.

Fulling a Knitted Swatch

All this talk of swatching, and I bet you're anxious to have your very own fulled swatch. You can use the following directions for testing any yarn for any pattern. Of course, if swatching for a pattern, you'll want to choose the appropriate yarn and needles for that particular pattern.

What Stitches Work Best

In most published knitting patterns that are destined to be fulled, you're most likely to encounter garter or stockinette. This could include stripes or intarsia or Fair-Isle color work. But, although you can certainly full cables or lacework, in many cases the fine details are too small to look like anything but a mistake. If you're dreaming of fuzzy felted cables or lace, just work a swatch first. What seems large and clunky at first may be just the perfect pattern to use in your dream project.

What You Need

- 10–20 yards of worsted-weight or Aran-weight yarn. Look for yarn that knits to 4.5–5 stitches per inch.
- US 10 / 6mm knitting needles
- Scissors
- Washing machine
- Small amount of laundry detergent
- Lingerie bag or zippered pillow case
- 2 to 3 old pillow cases for friction
- Disposable razor (optional)
- Notebook and pen

Swatch It Up

1. Cast on 16 stitches.
2. Work in stockinette stitch (knit one row, purl one row) until swatch is 4 inches from cast on.
3. Cast off.

Measurements and Notes

Before fulling your swatch, it's a good time to take some notes. Grab your felting or project notebook and write down the yarn name, color, and the measurement of the swatch in both stitches and rows. For the measurements, don't be tempted to estimate. Knowing the size before and after fulling will help you figure out the exact amount of shrinkage.

For example, in my case:

Yarn: Cascade 220, color 7814

Swatch size before fulling:

16 stitches by 18 rows

4 by 4 inch square

This way, you have something to compare to the après-fulling size of the swatch.

Shrink That Swatch

Now, you're ready to full. If working in a laundromat, make sure to use the same machine as you plan to use the next time. Different machines allow for different levels of agitation and wash temperature, and will provide different results.

1. Place the swatch inside the lingerie bag and zip the bag closed. Put it in the washing machine with the old pillowcases. Make sure to add just a little detergent; a tablespoon or two is enough.

2. Set the machine to hot wash with a cold water rinse on the lowest water level. If your machine has several cycles to choose from, select the roughest, longest, wash cycle. On some machines, this is labeled as *heavy duty* or *power wash*. Avoid anything that sounds too gentle; *lingerie* or *delicate* indicate a cycle that won't produce the agitation necessary.

3. Turn the machine on and wait. It's best practice to check the progress every 5 to 10 minutes of the wash cycle. (If using an industrial strength machine, you'll want to check even more often.) The fabric will first turn fuzzy and then will begin to shrink. For most pure wool yarns, you'll be able to continue to shrink until individual stitches are impossible to see. On a traditional top-loading machine, if the wash cycle has almost finished and the swatch can still continue to full, set the cycle back to the beginning and start again. Although it won't hurt the item to go through the rinse and spin cycles, it's a waste of time and energy until you're done fulling.

4. When you're happy with the finished size, take it out of the machine and let the machine finish the cycle as normal. Don't forget to dry the pillowcases and lingerie bag to prevent mildew.

Blocking

Notice that, when the swatch is wet, it's extremely pliable. You can tug in different directions to change the shape. For a swatch, you want the final shape to be as rectangular as possible. So, use your hands to pull and prod it into a nice, even shape. For a bag, hat, mitten, slipper, and so on, you can use a form to help block the piece into the right shape. For slippers, try

Front-Loader Felting

I'm lucky enough to have one of those fancy front-loading washing machines. It's incredibly gentle on my laundry, but isn't ideal for fulling. If you're in a similar situation, don't worry! You can absolutely full in a front-loader. It just takes a little longer, but to make up for the inefficiency, you're generally blessed with a smoother and more even finished product.

I set my machine to Power Wash on the longest wash cycle, with the lowest water level and fastest spin. I include a couple of pillow cases and otherwise follow the directions above. And then, I wait for the cycle to run through and the door to unlock.

For most yarns and most products, I need 2 or 3 full cycles. So, to make up for the wasted water, I do sometimes launder my sheets or non-terrycloth kitchen towels at the same time. Of course, dye from the projects has occasionally run onto the kitchen towels and old sheets, so I'll first use older items as a test.

placing your feet inside plastic shopping bags and then the still-wet slippers. If you can sit still for long enough, the slippers will be shaped to dry in the form of your foot. For a purse or pocket-like item, you can cover a book, box, or other stiff sided item with bags and insert into the purse to help stretch it and hold it in shape while drying.

To avoid mildew, make sure to let the piece dry in a well ventilated area, particularly if you live in a more humid climate. Mesh elevated drying racks, meant for sweaters, are handy to speed up the drying process. Also consider directing a fan towards the item as it dries, or setting it up in a breezy spot in your home. Most items will dry under these conditions within 12–24 hours.

Clean Up

After the swatch is dry, you have some choices to make. You can brush the wool with a wire brush to increase the furry appearance. You can leave it as is. You can take a disposable razor to the surface to groom and flatten. As you can see in the photo below, the shaved swatch is on the far right. There's no particular trick to doing this; just work until you're happy with the appearance. Don't be afraid to use scissors to cut off large fluffy bits. Whatever is quickest!

Final Measurements

You did all this work, so go ahead and measure the final dimensions of the fulled swatch. Is it now 2 inches tall and 3 inches wide? Is it larger or smaller? Every yarn and washing machine will provide a different finished texture and dimensions. There's no one right size, but keeping track of how swatches composed of

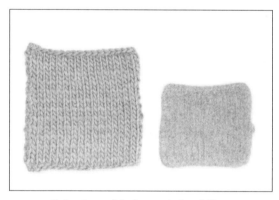

Knitted swatch before and after fulling.

different yarns work in your set up is incredibly helpful when working on items where the finished size matters. Remember, blocking when wet can help you obtain the size that you need.

I suggest labeling your swatches as well, using a piece of cardboard, yarn, and safety pin. Be sure to write down the yarn brand, needle size, and original size, in case it gets separated from your felting notebook where you've already recorded similar information. If you're concerned about rust stains, be sure to use rust-proof pins. Otherwise, wait until the swatch is completely dry before pinning.

Crochet ♥ Fulling Too

Die-hard hooking fanatics take note . . . crochet makes a gorgeous fulled fabric! Yes, it uses more yarn than knitting, but you're blessed with faster progress and a thicker fabric out of a skinnier yarn. Crochet is also better suited for lacey patterns or texture, even when fulling. Most of this is due to the larger size of the average crochet stitch. Since it's easier to make larger holes with chain stitches than with a knitted yarn over, it's possible to go crazy with lacey crochet and end up with a gorgeous fulled product.

With crochet, you'll also probably enjoy using an even larger hook than the needles you'd use for knitting. This helps the stitches open up more and makes for quicker fulling.

What You Need

- 20–30 yards of worsted or Aran weight yarn. Look for yarn that knits to 4.5–5 stitches per inch or crochets to 3 – 3.5 sc per inch.
- US K/10.5 6.5mm crochet hook
- Scissors
- Washing machine
- Small amount of laundry detergent
- Lingerie bag or zippered pillow case
- 2 to 3 old pillow cases for friction
- Disposable razor (optional)
- Notebook and pen

Swatch It Up

1. Chain 13.
2. Turn, work 12 single crochet across initial chain.
3. Continue to work rows of single crochet until swatch is 4 inches from chain.
4. Cut yarn and pull through.

Incidentally, you could work this swatch in half-double, double crochet, treble crochet, or any basic stitch. This is a fun experiment; try out a few different stitches and see how (and if) it impacts your finished swatch.

Measurements and Notes

Before actually fulling your swatch, it's a good time to take some notes. Grab your felting or project notebook and write down the yarn name, color, and the measurement of the swatch in both stitches and rows.

For example, in my case:

Yarn: Brown Sheep Lamb's Pride Bulky, color Old Rose
Swatch size before fulling:
12 stitches by 14 rows
Approximately 4 by 4 inch square

This way, you have something to compare to the après-fulling size of the swatch.

The Rest of the Work

Hey, the rest of the process is exactly the same as for the knitted swatch above! Go read through those directions, beginning with "Shrink That Swatch" on page 56.

Crocheted swatch before and after fulling.

Size Matters: The Problem with Shrinkage

By now, if you've fulled a swatch or two, you'll have noticed that switching yarns, hook, or needle sizes or using a different machine can all provide you with vastly different post-fulling measurements, even if your pre-fulling dimensions were identical.

This is the core problem with wet felting as well as fulling. Since you're creating something that's destined to shrink a certain amount, the final product is impacted by fiber content, space between fibers, thickness, and the fulling process. And, there's very little you can do to prevent this kind of size variation.

The best advice anyone can give is to be flexible when fulling. Know that the cute purse you're knitting may turn out an inch shorter and two inches wider than in the pattern. Know that sometimes patterns, such as the 'Junior' Varsity Jacket in chapter 7, will have you knit a yardage of fabric to be later cut into the right size and shape, in order to ensure proper fit.

For perfectly predictable results every time, follow these steps:

1. Do your swatching with the yarn and tools you expect to use. Determine the percentage of size the piece shrunk, both from side to side and from bottom to top. In general, a knitted piece will shrink dramatically more in row height than in stitch width, but even this may vary based on the above factors.

2. Assess the pattern to determine whether you'll need to make adjustments. If the pattern provides a pre-fulling gauge, this is fairly straightforward. Use the schematic diagram, if provided pre-fulling, to figure out the total number of rows in the piece. Then compare to the finished size.

   For example: If 100 rows gives you 20 inches of height according to the pattern, but your swatch is telling you that 20 rows gives 3 inches, you can figure out that if you knit the project as is, you'll end up with something 5 inches too short. To compensate, find the part of the pattern without increases or decreases and add enough rows to get you closer to the right measurements. In this case, you'd need approximately 134 rows. So, you'll need to find the right place to add 34 rows.

Now, this is a fairly dramatic example. Chances are, if you use the same yarn suggested or make your substitution as close as possible, your results will be much closer to the recommended finished size.

Get as math-geeky as you want to and figure out how to adjust the pattern before fulling. Or, stay cool and know you'll be thrilled with whatever comes out and that most small issues can be fixed with a little blocking. The choice is up to you!

Recycled Felt: Even Bad Knits Get a Second Chance

If recent books and magazine articles are any indication, the next big trend in garment crafting is the concept of customizing or recycling clothing. This trend is even cooler when applied to fulling. Even the ugliest, poorest fitting sweater can live a second, more appreciated life, after fulling.

The concept is simple. Find a pure wool or shrinkable blend sweater and shrink it in the machine with the directions earlier in the chapter. Then, after it's shrunk into the right type of fabric, cut it with scissors and sew it into something else. Although it helps to have a sewing machine, you can also do this by hand!

Recycled felt is the ultimate in instant gratification. The piece is already knitted . . . you just have to wait for a machine cycle or two and then you get to have fun crafting something new. Most recycled projects take a single evening or afternoon. Even better, if you're savvy at the thrift store, your material cost will be ultra low. Grabbing a pure wool vintage sweater for $10 is vastly different than buying the yarn to make the sweater in the first place. If working from scratch, you'd spend at least $50 for an adult-sized pullover.

So, along with the lower price tag comes a much lower sensation of risk. If a recycled sweater doesn't work out as the first idea you had, you can always turn it into something else or put it aside for later. No harm, no foul, and only an afternoon spent on the experiment. Get creative, and have fun!

Tips for Thrift-Store Shopping

In chapter 1, we covered the burn test for determining whether a fiber is wool or acrylic. Unfortunately, most thrift stores don't look kindly on taking a match to their goods. So, you're best off to look for well-labeled items. Unless the labels have been ripped out, any originally store-bought sweater should have a tag indicating fiber content and care instructions. Just as when yarn shopping, you want to look for "Pure Virgin Wool," "New Wool," or similar. Avoid anything that says you can safely machine wash.

Sweaters that have sparkly bits, beads, or are made partially from materials that are visibly *not* from an animal can be fun to work with; just as with blended yarns, they can yield different results than expected.

If planning to felt into a you-sized garment, such as our Menswear For You vest and Cropped Cardigan in chapter 7, seek out items that are quite a bit larger than your usual size. In fact, buy as big as you can. The price is usually the same as for smaller sizes, and although you can always cut out excess fabric and reseam after fulling, you can't make a piece larger.

When using sweater pieces for accessories, size isn't as important. Still, it's usually more cost-effective to buy big.

Other Sources for Sweaters

When in doubt, check your closet or the closet of a friend or relative. Chances are, you have at least one ill-fitting or worn-out wool sweater that could use a new life as a throw pillow or handbag. If you're a knitter, you may have some finished (or almost finished) sweaters that you know you'll never rip out and reknit or finish. They may be too small; the yarn may have pilled horribly; or you may just absolutely hate the style.

For proof that you can sometimes make a silk purse from a sow's ear, check out the Cropped Cardigan in chapter 7. My original handknit sweater always fit fantastically, but the yarn, a blend of wool and angora, shed everywhere I went, leaving a thick hairy trail of hot-pink angora on everything from my desk chair to my favorite bra. So, one afternoon, I threw it in the wash to see what would happen. The yarn fulled nicely, controlling the angora completely. Et voila! A shed-free, just as luxurious cropped cardigan.

A final bonus to using your own failed knit projects as fodder for the fulling pile. . . you always know the fiber will (or won't) felt.

Basic Sewing Tips for Working with Felt

Teaching you how to operate a sewing machine is a bit outside the scope of the book. If you're interested in the art of quilting, crafting your own clothing with fabric, or even tailoring existing clothes, consider picking up a reference book or registering for a basic sewing course through your local community college or sewing store.

However, to work with recycled felt, you don't need much sewing knowledge or experience.

Choose the Right Needle and Thread

It's essential to fit your machine with a suitable needle. Wool felt is typically pretty thick and tough, so choose a needle recommended for heavy denim, leather, or upholstery fabric. You'll want pretty sturdy cotton thread as well.

Don't Worry About Finishing Seams and Edges

Since the wool has already been fulled and will be unlikely to unravel, you don't have to worry much about finishing the inside of your seams. So, focus on sewing a straight seam and then use a steam iron to press open. A half-inch seam allowance is plenty for most purposes. Anything more on a garment, and you'll have ultra-bulky seams.

For raw, cut edges, instead of worrying about hems, just make straight cuts. For a more arty appeal, choose a decorative scissors. Pinking shears make classic sawtooth edges, but scrapbooking stores often sell wavy blades as well as plastic cutting templates for more complex designs.

Measure Twice, Cut Once

It's a bit of a cliché in the sewing world, but measure at least twice to prevent making an unrecoverable error in cutting. Use a non-bendy yard stick and rotary cutter for the most precision. Dressmaker's chalk is also good for drawing where you intend to cut so you can check for fit while changes can still be made.

Keep It Simple

Whether sewing on the machine or by hand, keep it as simple as possible if you're just learning. Simple seams should be straightforward enough. Adding a zipper, pleats, or refashioning a sleeve is quite a bit more challenging. Feel up to the task? Go for it! With recycled felt, you've likely only invested a few dollars anyhow.

Be Craftily Creative

In part because fulling pre-knit sweaters is addictively fun, recycled felt is a fun and easy way to experiment with different techniques. This book only explores a few of them. Check out Shannon Okey's Octopillow in chapter 9 for her take on applying Shibori tying techniques before fulling the fabric, or the recycled needle roll in chapter 8 for a nice way of blending quilting patchwork style with cozy fulled knits.

You can get inspiration from anywhere: fashion television to art school publications. Have fun and experiment. This book is a great place to begin but don't be afraid to explore further! Use these projects as the perfect starting point.

Troubleshooting and Tips

No matter how long you've been "full of it," you may run into trouble from time to time. These tips should help you avoid problems before you start.

Edge Flare

Have you noticed, on your knit swatches, that the cast-off edges tend to flare? No amount of care with your tension will prevent this. By nature of the fabric, the cast-off edge will stay a little fatter than the rest after fully fulling. (Say that five times fast!)

To compensate for this after fulling, you can block out the piece by pinning it down into a square shape and letting dry. But many patterns take this into account during the design process. It's not uncommon to see the edgings worked with slightly fewer stitches than the body of the piece. If you see increases or decreases done in a single row just before or after an edging, this is the reason. It looks weird and exaggerated, but once fulled, it gives nice shaping to the object.

Unraveling Ends

One of fulling's big attractions is that ends don't need to be wound in that tightly, at least not compared to normal knitting or crochet. The fulling process erases a lot of tension blips and other mistakes, including less-than-stellar woven ends. When switching balls, you can even just tie a knot!

Don't spend much time weaving ends. Instead, just loosely sew them in one direction. Each end should take less than 30 seconds. Taking a little bit of time to make them more secure prevents disastrous unraveling in the wash.

Stubborn Fullers

Some yarns are notoriously slow to full, despite being 100 percent wool. Chalk it up to the dye process, the spin, or just the way it's been processed; this happens all the time. Noro's delightful Kureyon is perpetually a hesitant fuller. Have you run your project through the wash several times? Is it getting smaller, but are you still able to see the stitches? Chances are, it can be fulled even further.

Take a note from the wet felters out there. Wool needs to be shocked to shrink. Try plunging the item in a bucket of ice water and then in a bucket of near-boiling water. Repeat this a few times, and you should see some changes.

When in doubt, just keep going. It may feel like a small eternity, but any of the yarns listed in this book, will felt down to the point where individual stitches are tough, even impossible, to see.

Make Sure It's Hot

For the best results in fulling, the water must be exceptionally hot. Some houses have temperature-controlled water heaters to prevent scalding of delicate skin in the shower. You can either change the setting temporarily, or, if you have a top-loader, you can even add a bit of boiling water while the tub is filling.

When interrupting the cycle to start again from the beginning of the wash cycle, check to see that the water is hot enough. If not, you'll want to let the tub drain and start fresh with super-hot water.

Watch Your Gauge

Although many patterns say that exact gauge is unimportant for fulling, that particular advice is a bit misleading. Although the difference between 2 and 2.125 stitches per inch probably doesn't matter much, you still want to be close to the recommended gauge to give your project the best shot of ending up the same size as indicated. So, do work a gauge swatch to make sure you are using the right needles or hooks. And hey, once you've done a gauge swatch, you might as well full it!

Swatch, Swatch, Swatch!

Are you sick of reading about this yet? Tough luck! Swatching all the way through the drying process lets you catch many problems before they become irreversible. I doubt you want to spend weeks and $100 on supplies for a project just to toss it into the back of your closet, never to be seen again. So, please make a fulled swatch. It's good for you.

Cast On and Off Loosely

Make sure to cast on and off very, very loosely. Some knitters find it helpful to switch to a needle several sizes larger to force a bit of looseness. This goes for crochet, too. Make sure that initial chain is fairly loose!

Chapter Five

◆

Dying to Dye

Does your personality type lean slightly toward A? Would your friends describe you as a die-hard control freak? Chances are, you'll love creating your own custom colors for use with felting. Although it takes a little more effort, when you dye your own, you'll be able to get the right color or colors for your next project. Take a little dye, a little vinegar, some water, and heat, and conquer the color wheel!

Why Dye?

Put quite simply, dyeing white fiber or yarn puts you in control. You're no longer limited by the selection available online or in your local store. You no longer have to shell out big bucks for hand-painted fiber to obtain that spectacular marble effect when wet felting. Need just a little bit of red merino? You can dye as little or as much as you want. Sure, there's no instant gratification. The dye process itself takes a few hours, and then there's the drying time. But, spend a Saturday dyeing some wool and you'll be set for as many projects as you can dream up.

The following pages give you a quick and dirty introduction to the art of dyeing from a non-controlled perspective. Although you can use scales and precise measurements to dye in a way that's predictable and repeatable, this usually exceeds the patience levels of most home dyers. If you want to get serious about DYO (dye your own), I suggest you invest in a more technical manual of dye techniques, such as the volumes available from Interweave Press. Particularly helpful to me while beginning to experiment with nonfood safe dyes was *Hands On Dyeing* by Betsy Blumenthal and Kathryn Kreider.

Acid Dyes

From Kool-Aid drink powder sold in supermarkets, to the harder to find acid dyes, you have a choice in materials. Some dyes are meant for use with cotton or synthetic fabrics. Some dyes are possible to use on multiple fiber types. Others effectively work on only protein fibers, such as wool or silk.

Since this is a felting book, and felting requires protein fibers, such as wool, this chapter will focus on acid dyes. For working with drink powders or even icing dyes, check out the sidebar below on kid- (and klutz-) friendly dyeing.

Acid dyes are named so because they require some kind of acid—in our case, white vinegar—to help set the dye. Several major fiber art companies currently produce and sell acid dyes. They typically are found in powdered, or crystalline, form and can be purchased as pre-blended colors—such as lilac, rose, maroon, or lime—or in sets of primary colors red, yellow, and blue. If you choose to purchase the primaries, plus black, you can create your own color blend. For many home dyers, it's quicker and more predictable to simply buy the pre-blended powders in the colors they choose.

Kool-Aid: Not Just for Cults and Kids

For an easy and safe introduction to common dye techniques, consider dyeing wool with Kool-Aid or other powdered drink mixes. This technique is great for stitch n' bitch parties or for kids. The wool gets a little stinky, but it's fun to see what develops!

Want to dye with icing dye, such as Wilton coloring? You can use exactly the same instructions.
What you'll need:

- ◆ Protein-based yarn, such as pure wool, tied into skeins. (If the yarn is balled, wind into a loose skein by wrapping around the back of a chair.) While you can dye as much (or as little) as you'd like, stick with a skein or two the first time you try it out.
- ◆ Several packages of unsweetened Kool-Aid or other unsweetened drink mix. If the mix contains any sugar or artificial sweetener, you'll end up with a sticky un-dyed mess. Look for mixes that contain instructions for adding sugar, and you'll be fine. You'll need approximately 1 package per ounce of yarn. Dye all the yarn a single color or pick multiple colors for a hand-painted look.
- ◆ 1 large pot and steamer basket, with lid, large enough to hold your skeins
- ◆ Turkey baster or wide paintbrush for applying Kool-Aid
- ◆ Large plastic bag of any kind
- ◆ Cups or mugs, 1 for each color
- ◆ Plastic or latex gloves for each participant

continued

continued

Steps to dying wool with Kool-Aid:

1. Before beginning to dye, place your yarn in the sink and wash it lightly with a bit of mild soap or detergent (the soap helps set the color). Rinse gently.

2. Lay the skeins on top of the plastic bag on a hard surface, such as a kitchen counter. Put each color of Kool-Aid into a separate cup and add water, two tablespoons for each packet. Mix well.

3. Use the turkey baster to suck up some of the mix and squirt it carefully over the yarn. Be sure to rinse the baster between colors. If using a paintbrush, use the brush to liberally apply the mix. If your skeins are quite large, you may need to use your hands to work the dye through the entire skein.
   Be careful when adding multiple colors; the dye will bleed slightly at any areas that overlap and may turn the wool a muddy color.

4. After the skeins are fully dyed, add water to the large pot, making sure the water level is below the beginning of the steamer basket. Heat the pot to boiling, then turn the burner off. Place the yarn in the steamer basket and cover, steaming for 45–60 minutes. Remove the basket and let cool in an empty sink.

5. When the yarn is room temperature, wash it gently in room-temperature water using mild soap. (Note: Using water that's too cold or too hot could cause the wool to felt.) Rinse the last of the soap and dye out of the yarn, squeeze to remove as much water as possible, and hang to dry.

   You can also use your microwave to set the dye. Just wrap the skeins tightly in plastic wrap, place in a microwave-safe casserole dish, and heat for 2 or 3 minutes. Check to make sure the liquid is running clear. If not, heat again until it does. Rinse and dry as directed above.

If you are just starting to experiment with dyes, consider buying a set of primaries, plus a few well-chosen colors from elsewhere on the color wheel. Love lime? How about purple? These might be good ones to start with. Although you can blend your own from yellow and blue, or blue and red, you'll save time and be able to start dyeing a color you love immediately.

Tools of the Trade: What You Need to Get Started

Most of the cost involved in dyeing is one time only. Although you will need to replace dye, vinegar, and, of course, fiber, these things are typically quite inexpensive compared to buying pre-dyed fiber in the shop. The equipment listed in this section and the instructions later in the chapter cover what I use to dye fiber and yarn at home. The brand of dye you purchase may include slightly different instructions. When in doubt, go for what the dye tells you.

Note: Because dyeing with acid dye powder is a messy process, and involves some safety concerns, I recommend having a *completely separate set of dyeing equipment* from what you use around the house or for cooking. Any dye or dye powder involves chemicals that can make you extremely ill if you inhale or ingest them. Towels and clothes may get stained, so only use what you can stand to ruin in this way. Any food- or cooking-related equipment may be tempting to use from your kitchen stores. However, even in the case of the salt and vinegar, you don't want to ever cook with or ingest anything that's come into contact with the mixed dye. Spend a couple of extra bucks and make sure it's entirely separate from your kitchen stash. More safety information can be found in the next section.

- **Fiber, Fabric, or Yarn** To dye, you absolutely, positively need something to dye. That's pretty obvious, right? When just getting started working with heat dye techniques, I'd suggest starting with yarn or fabric. Remember to select fiber made from protein sources: wool, alpaca, silk, angora, or cashmere all work fine. If dyeing roving, you'll need to be especially careful to not accidentally felt the wool during dyeing. Read more about accidental felting in the sidebar later in this chapter.

- **Dye Powders** Even one color of acid dye powder is enough. Of course, that will give you only one color of fiber. Consider starting with at least the three primaries: yellow, blue, and red. From these, you can mix any color at all. Adding a black dye will allow you to create darker shades. Alternatively, buy a few of your favorite pre-mixed colors.

- **Acid and Salt** Stronger acids are available, but for the home dyer, nothing is better than plain old white vinegar. Go to a superstore and pick up a large 2-liter bottle of branded white vinegar strictly for dye use, as you'll need several cups full each time you dye.

  Table salt acts as a *leveling agent* and helps make the dye adhere to the fiber more completely and evenly. Again, purchase a separate box of salt strictly for use when dyeing.

- **Covered Stock Pot with Steamer Insert** Look for a stainless steel stock pot (with a well-fitting lid) in as large of a volume as you can find. Canning pots or large pasta pots will work nicely. If the pot comes with a steamer or pasta basket designed to hang inside, you'll be easily able to dye in multiple colors. Just make sure there's at least 2 inches of space between the bottom of the steamer and the bottom of the pot to allow room for simmering water. Expect to pay $40 to $60 for the pot set at a housewares store. You can save some cash by shopping around at garage sales or thrift stores.

- **Measuring Supplies** Even if you're not completely concerned about precision and predictability, you'll still need some basic measuring supplies. Grab sets of measuring spoons and cups marked with both imperial and metric measurements. If you have to choose, go for metric. Most acid dyes are produced in metric standard countries, so the rest of this chapter will speak in metric terms. If you need to do the conversions to imperial, check out the sidebar later in this chapter.

You'll also need a glass liquid measuring cup for larger amounts. Try for a larger cup that will hold up to 8 cups of water, or 2 liters. Smaller liquid measures with a spout for easy pouring are helpful for applying dye.

Remember, you're only going to use these for dyeing; not cooking.

◆ Closeable Jars or Containers for Storing Dyes If you plan on premixing several powdered dyes into stock solutions, you'll need some containers to keep them in for next time. Look for glass or sturdy plastic bottles that can close completely, both to prevent spills and to keep things safe. If the bottle openings are fairly small, also buy a plastic funnel for ease in filling the bottles.

◆ Stirrers and Tongs A few cheap wooden spoons for stirring and a set of metal or heat-resistant tongs, such as those used for the grill come in handy when working with the wet fiber. Again, these should be used only for dyeing.

◆ Soap Before and after dyeing, the fiber or yarn will need to be gently washed. Gentle laundry detergent is fine for this. You'll also want to work either in a sink or a washtub.

◆ Safety Gear For your own safety, wear old clothing, get a pair of thick rubber gloves, and wear a face mask when working with dyes. Read more on safety in the next section. It's really important, so please don't be tempted to skip over it!

◆ Other Handy Stuff It's great to keep newspapers, old towels, and plastic bags on hand for quick clean up. I prefer to use old bath towels than can be washed and reused rather than go through rolls and rolls of paper towels every time I dye. For presoaking fiber, a stoppable sink, glass bowl, or washtub comes in handy. A kitchen timer is a great help for figuring out when everything's finished. For hand-painted yarns and fiber, turkey basters or paintbrushes can be used to apply dye to specific areas. Plastic wrap is also essential for hand-paints. If you want to keep track of your dye experiments, keep a notebook and pen nearby. For drying, plastic clothes hangers can be hung in your shower, allowing the clean dyed fiber to drip dry.

Safety First

Dyes, particularly those sold in powdered form, can be hazardous to work with. Inhaling or ingesting the powder, even when you use powdered drink mixes, can lead to several health problems. Whenever working with dyes, do use the following guidelines to keep everything as safe as possible.

Safe Dyers Cover Up

Keep a separate set of clothing to wear while dyeing. Just as you want to prevent staining your skin, you also want to keep any chemical assistants off of your skin. Tie your hair out of the way so you're not tempted to brush aside a stray strand while your gloved hands are messy.

Wear rubber gloves and at minimum a surgical face mask, if not a respirator, when mixing stock solutions. Even though you're unlikely to splatter dye if you're being careful, protective eyewear, or at least a set of clear fashion glasses, ensures that your eyes remain safe from flare-ups.

Make a Dye Box

Just as you might have prepared a box for your wet felting kit, do the same for your dye equipment. Instead of using your good stock pot for both dyeing and preparing that killer tomato sauce, use it for one purpose or the other. *Never ever use your dye equipment for cooking, or vice versa.* Don't forget to also set aside measuring cups and spoons and any storage containers. Carefully label all dyes and chemicals. Keep a separate container of vinegar and salt in this box as well. Even if your kitchen is out of salt, don't be tempted to dig into this stash. It's not worth the risk. After your box is assembled, find a safe storage area that's far from kids and pets.

Set Up Your Dye Area (and Clean Up After)

It's not always possible for the home dyer to have a dedicated dyeing area. Since you need a heat source and water supply, most occasional dyers end up working in the kitchen. If this sounds like your situation, be especially careful to clean up both before and after you dye. Keep any non-dyers, especially kids and pets, out of the room until after everything is completely clean.

Before you dye, store all kitchen equipment away in cupboards or closets. This includes things like your salt and pepper shakers, dishcloths, fruit bowls, and any dishes or utensils that usually sit out and exposed. The idea is to keep your eating stuff as separate from your dyeing stuff as possible. If you're working in a small apartment with limited storage space, clean off your kitchen counters and table and temporarily move everything to another room. To prevent staining, cover all work surfaces with newspaper or drop cloths. Just remember to keep these things away from the stove.

Clean up when you're done. Wash all your equipment and store it in your dye box. Then, when everything is put away, thoroughly scour all kitchen surfaces with heavy-duty cleaners, including the stove top and sink.

Stay Focused

It may sound obvious, but do not be tempted to crack open a beer or diet soda while working with dye. Eating or drinking while working with dye is just asking for trouble. Remember, this is stuff that you don't want inside you. Although most acid dyes are technically non-toxic, the chemicals that accompany them can break down into nasty stuff inside your body. I'll spare you the gory details, but there was an episode in Sudan a few decades back where dye chemicals entered the food supply. . . .

In the same way, don't walk away from your dye area and keep an eye on what's going on at all times. Be especially careful of pets and little ones. You don't want to expose their little bodies to any of this stuff, either.

Be safe; stay focused on what you're doing at all times.

Avoid "Easy" Dye Shortcuts

Articles online or in DIY magazines may suggest dyeing in your microwave or dishwasher. Although you can do this with reasonable safety when using powdered drink mix or food dye, please avoid this when working with acid dyes. Even though the risk level is low if you're careful, do you really want these chemicals heating up in equipment that you use to prepare food or sanitize dishes? If you want to try microwave dyeing, do it with Kool Aid, following the directions earlier in this chapter. Or, get a second, used microwave to hook up just when you dye. Otherwise, stick to the stove top and a dye-specific stock pot. It works just as well and almost as quickly.

Is the Effort Worth It?

Sound like a lot of work? Do the safety precautions recommended scare you off? Don't let them until you try it once. Take a spare afternoon and try it out. You may love it. Also, most home dyers only dye occasionally in large batches. Doing a lot of work at once makes the effort more worthwhile.

Conversions for Dyers

Most acid dyes are produced outside of the United States and use metric measurements on instructions and packaging. If possible, try to obtain a set of measuring spoons and cups with metric measurements. If you need to perform the conversions from milliliters (ml) to teaspoons, tablespoons, and cups, check out the following chart. These values are "close-enough" approximations.

5 ml = 1 teaspoon
15 ml = 1 Tablespoon
50 ml = $\frac{1}{4}$ cup
100 ml = $\frac{7}{16}$ cup
200 ml = $\frac{7}{8}$ cup
250 ml = 1 cup
1 L = 4 $\frac{1}{4}$ cups

Mixing Stock Solutions

Since most acid dye is sold in powdered form, for the most even and consistent dyeing it should be dissolved in water before using. This is called creating a *stock solution*. Storing dye as stock solutions is easy, safe, and convenient since dye is at its most hazardous when in powdered form.

The instructions provided here are appropriate for most types of acid dyes. If your dye powder came with instructions detailing different levels of dilution, use those measurements instead. These instructions also cover mixing a solution from a single color of dye, rather than creating your own blends of multiple primary colors. A few hints have been included for mixing your own colors.

This process can take up to an hour. Make sure that you allow for time to clean up.

What You Need

- Acid dye, in powdered form
- Measuring spoons
- Liquid measuring cups; small (2 cup / 500ml) and large (8 cup / 2L)
- Glass or plastic storage bottle, with lids
- Funnel, if the openings to the storage bottle are small
- Wood or plastic spoon for stirring
- Label and pen for marking details of stock solution
- Face mask or respirator
- Rubber or thick latex gloves
- Old clothing
- Protective eyewear
- Newspaper
- Cleaning supplies

Getting Ready: Your Work Area, Your Supplies, and You

Most importantly, your work area needs to be safe, both during and after mixing the stock solution. Choose a well-ventilated but non-breezy area. The idea is to have complete control over the dye powder at all times. Many home dyers work in the bathtub, laying down dampened newspapers on all surfaces to help catch any loose dye.

You should also wear old clothing, gloves, and a face mask at all times. Tie hair off your face as much as possible. Protective glasses may feel geeky, but you don't want this stuff in or near your eyes.

Before beginning, gather all supplies in your work area. If you don't already know the volume of your storage containers, take some time to figure it out. An easy way to estimate the volume is to fill the container with water, then empty into your large liquid measuring container. Find the next lowest measurement line and make a note of what it says in either cups or milliliters. You want to mix enough stock solution to only come to this line to make sure that it all fits in one of your bottles.

Mixing the Solution

First, you need to determine how much dye powder you'll need for the volume of stock solution. Speaking generically, most acid dyes recommend somewhere around 5ml (1 teaspoon) of dye to 200ml (⅞ cup) of water. To determine how much dye you'll need for your storage containers, take the volume of the container in milliliters (cups) and divide by 200ml (⅞ cup). Then, multiply by 5ml (1 teaspoon). It may be easiest to adjust the volume of stock solution to obtain an even measurement of dye powder.

For example, let's say that my container holds a liter of water. Perfect! I'll need to add an even 25ml of dye powder. But, if my container holds 700ml, according to the formula, I'd need to add 17.5ml of dye powder. Since I don't have a half milliliter measure, I'd choose to round down to 15ml of dye powder and 600ml of water. Be sure to make a note of the amount of water you'll need.

Working in your larger liquid measuring cup, carefully spoon the required amount of dye powder. If blending colors at this point, such as adding two or more primary colors together, measure the desired amounts of each color but be sure to end up with the total amount of dye powder as already determined.

Next, add a small amount of hot water and stir into a paste-like mixture. When the paste has been thoroughly mixed, gradually continue adding water while stirring until the stock solution reaches the total volume according to formula.

Carefully pour the dye into a storage bottle, label the bottle, and rinse off any equipment. If mixing more than one color, continue on to the next color.

Shelf Life

When labeling your stock solutions, don't forget to include the date the dye was mixed. Most acid dyes have a useful shelf life of less than 6 months before the strength of the dye deteriorates. For the longest (and safest) life, store in a cool, dark location, out of reach of kids and pets.

Your First Acid Dye Trip: Single Color Dyeing

Got some white yarn or wool fiber? Got your dye kit together? You're ready to go. For this activity, be sure to have at least 4 hours free. The amount of stock solution recommended should create a medium color tone. For lighter color, use less dye. For darker color, use more.

What You Need

- 500g (1 lb) of fiber or skeins of yarn. (If you want to dye less, you'll need less dye, vinegar, and water than indicated.)
- Single color of acid dye, already mixed into a stock solution. See previous section for instructions.
- White vinegar—500ml (2 cups)
- Table salt—75ml (5 Tablespoons)
- Measuring cups and spoons

- Stirring spoons
- Large stock pot with lid. The steamer basket is not necessary for this exercise.
- Glass bowl or casserole dish from dyeing kit. You won't want to use this for cooking.
- Tongs
- Rubber or thick latex gloves
- Old clothing
- Clock or kitchen timer
- Detergent
- Stove top or electric burner hot enough to boil water
- Plastic coat hangers, for drying

Acid Dyeing Instructions

Now you're ready to dye! Follow these steps:

1. You'll need to presoak the fiber. Do this by gently washing it with detergent in luke-warm water. Rinse and let it sit in the water until it's thoroughly saturated.

2. Prepare your dye pot: To your stock pot, add 15L of water, 250ml of stock solution, and 75ml of salt. Stir well to mix. Add the wet fiber to the pot.

3. Place the pot on the stove, cover, and bring gradually to a gentle boil over medium heat. Continue to simmer on low for 30 minutes, stirring frequently.

4. Using the tongs, remove the fiber from the dye pot and set it in the spare bowl or casserole dish. Add half of the vinegar to the dye pot and stir again to mix.

5. Replace the fiber in the dye pot and continue to simmer for 15 minutes, stirring often.

6. Again remove the fiber and add the remaining vinegar, stirring again. By adding the vinegar in two stages, you are more evenly distributing the acid on the fiber. Replace the fiber and continue to simmer for a further 15 minutes.

7. Remove the dye pot from the heat and allow to cool gradually to room temperature. Remove the fiber and rinse with lukewarm water until the water runs clear.

8. Add a little bit of gentle detergent and wash gently. Rinse again and hang to dry. I like to hang my fiber from plastic clothes hangers in my shower. This lets the water drip away. Since the rinse water ran clear earlier, you shouldn't be risking dyeing your shower floor. If you're concerned, or are dyeing at your mom's house, maybe consider placing a clean but dyeable towel on the floor under the dripping fiber. Most yarns and fibers take about 24 hours to fully dry. You can speed things up by letting them dry outside, provided the weather cooperates.

Save the Felting for Later

Loosely spun wool yarn and wool roving can accidentally felt during the dye process. You can probably guess why; all that stirring and hot water is the perfect recipe for felt. Although only a lot of care and attention can prevent accidental felting, these three tips don't hurt!

- **Stir very, very carefully.** When you must, stir the fiber slowly and gently. When you have to stir to mix the contents of the dye pot, remove the fiber first. If the dye pot contents are fully mixed, just immersing the fiber will be enough to evenly distribute the dye on the fiber.
- **Consider hand-dyeing, even for solid colors.** Steaming yarn that has been already saturated with dye can be a more gentle dyeing process and help avoid felting. Read ahead into the "Hand-paint Heaven" section for details.
- **Clean carefully.** When washing and rinsing the fiber, you want to always match the water temperature to the temperature of the fiber. If the fiber is still hot, use hot water. If the fiber is room temperature, use water that feels lukewarm. Remember, shocking the fiber with a dramatic temperature change is one of the quickest ways to felt.

Hand-paint Heaven

Multiple colors of dye added by hand to a skein of yarn or roving is called *hand painting.* This is an addictively fun way to get a little crazy color into your felting projects. The process is similar to the single color dye technique previously explained. But, this time you'll apply the dye before it goes into the pot. You'll also use a steamer basket instead of adding the fiber directly to the water.

What You Need

- 250g (½ lb) of fiber or loosely tied skeins of yarn. (If you want to dye less, you'll need less dye, vinegar, and water than indicated.)
- Several colors of stock solutions. You'll need a total of 125ml of dye to fully saturate the fiber.
- White vinegar—250ml (1 cup)
- Table salt—125ml (½ cup)
- Measuring cups and spoons
- Stirring spoons

- Large stock pot with lid and steamer basket.
- Glass bowl or spare pot large enough to hold 7L of water and fiber at the same time
- Plastic-covered counter, large enough to hold the fiber. A low-rimmed cookie sheet can work nicely. Just be sure to never again use it for cooking.
- Plastic wrap
- Tongs
- Rubber or thick latex gloves
- Old clothing
- Clock or kitchen timer
- Detergent
- Stove top or electric burner hot enough to boil water
- Plastic coat hangers, for drying

Hand-painting Instructions

1. Prepare your work area by doing the following: On the plastic-covered counter, lay out lengths of plastic wrap long enough for your fiber or skeins of yarn to sit on comfortably with plenty of room. This wrap will be folded over the fiber to prevent colors from bleeding together later on, so you may want to do a test run to make sure that you can easily enclose the fiber in the wrap.

2. Now, you'll want to presoak the fiber. Gently wash and rinse the fiber in lukewarm water. Add the white vinegar, table salt, and 15L of water to your glass bowl or spare pot. Mix well and add the fiber. Let soak for at least 15 minutes to completely saturate the fiber.

3. Remove the fiber from the presoak solution, squeezing slightly to remove excess liquid, and place on the center of the plastic wrap.

4. By squeezing the dye out of the mix bottles, apply each color of dye separately in bands or sections, making sure to keep a little un-dyed fiber in between color areas. Use your gloved hands to squeeze the dye thoroughly into the fiber. This will also let the dye spread out and will help cover the un-dyed areas. When first experimenting with multiple dye colors, it can be easiest to work with only two or three colors. It's also best to add just a little of the dye at a time, rather than risk a lot of dripping. Turn the fiber over to make sure the dye is penetrating all the way through. If not, apply more dye on this side in the same way. When dyeing, the best rule is to use just as much as you need. Start slowly; you can always add more. Ideally, you shouldn't have any spare dye on the work area that wasn't able to be absorbed by the wool. If you do, use a sponge, old towel, or paper towels to clean up.

5. When you are finished applying the dye, fold over all sides of the plastic wrap to completely cover the dyed fiber without rearranging the fiber in any way. If you find you need more plastic wrap to do the job, add it now. The wrap needs to be in place to prevent the dye from leaking and bleeding into other colors. When the wrap is fully in place, fold the plastic-enclosed fiber in half a few times until it will fit in the steamer basket.

6. Place the dye pot on the stove and fill with water to well below the steamer basket. Heat to boiling. Carefully add the plastic-wrapped fiber to the steamer basket. Put the lid on and simmer slowly for 45 minutes. Make sure that the water doesn't boil away entirely. If it gets low, remove the steamer basket and add more water.

7. Remove the dye pot from the heat and allow it to cool gradually to room temperature. Unwrap the plastic from around the yarn or fiber and wash carefully in the sink with lukewarm water and gentle detergent. Rinse until water runs clear. Hang to dry.

An Overview of Overdyeing

Of course, the preceding techniques can be used to overdye a batch of previously colored fiber, fabric, or yarn. You can also dye previously felted items. Just be aware that adding color to a previously colored item will blend the two colors together. For example, dyeing a light blue felted scarf with a red dye should turn the scarf slightly purple in tone. If possible, test on a sample first, or prepare yourself for redyeing into black or dark brown later on if the color doesn't work out the way you hope.

For a great example of overdyed felt, check out Shannon Okey's Octopillow in chapter 9. Before beginning any dye project, please do read through this entire chapter again before starting the project!

◆ Part Two ◆

Patterns and Projects

Chapter Six

◆◆◆

Never Too Many Bags

The Ultra-Simple One-Night Bag

Double stranded yarn and big, big needles make this bag a true "one-night stand."

I'm On the Case

Carry your baby (or feminine) essentials in style with this snazzy case.

Ah! Savasana! Yoga Mat Bag

Just breathe with this knit yoga tote.

Some Assembly Required

Simple crochet wallet embellished with cute buttons.

Holy Smokes! (A Holey Tote)

This tote uses an easier than imagined cast-on and cast-off pattern to create a unique structure.

The Ultra-Simple One-Night Bag

If you've knit a scarf, you'll have no problem working this simple bag. This design uses two strands of yarn and big needles to get you fulling as quickly as possible. As shown, I used one strand of a self-striping wool and one strand of a solid-colored yarn to create the subtle striping effect.

Project Rating: Flirtation

Cost: $30

Necessary Skills: knitting and purling (page 192); fulling in the machine (page 50)

Techniques:

K1fb Insert right needle into stitch and knit, but do not remove stitch from left needle; bring the right needle around to the back of the stitch and knit into the back of the stitch; drop stitch from left needle. One stitch has been increased

K2tog Knit the next two stitches together

4-Stitch I-Cord Using a double-pointed needle, CO 4 sts. K 1 row.

Next Row Instead of turning work around to work back on the WS, slide all sts to other end of needle, switch needle back to your left hand, bring yarn around back of work, and start knitting the sts again. I-Cord is worked with the RS facing at all times.

Repeat this row to form I-Cord. After a few rows, work will begin to form a tube.

Finished Size after Fulling

Length: 13 inches
Width: 7 inches
Strap Length: 15 inches

Materials

- MC: Noro Kureyon (50g, 109 yd/100m, 100 percent wool), color 54–2 balls
- CC: Cascade 220 (100g, 220 yd/200m, 100 percent wool), color 8393–1 skein
- Substitution: Approximately 218 yd/200m each of two types of worsted weight feltable wool. You'll need 436 yd/400m total.
- US 17/12mm straight needles
- 1 set US 17/12mm double-pointed needles
- Yarn needle
- 1 large button
- Sewing thread to match yarn
- Sewing needle

Instructions

Note: Yarn is held doubled throughout.

Using straight needles and one strand each of MC and CC held together, CO 35 sts.

K 2 rows.

Next Row [RS]: K3, kfb, [k6, kfb] 4 times, k3. 40 sts.

Work in stockinette st until work measures 30 inches, ending with a WS row.

Next Row [RS]: K3, k2tog, [k6, k2tog] 4 times, k3. 35 sts.

K 2 rows. BO all sts.

Strap

Using double-pointed needles and one strand each of MC and CC held together, work 4-st I-Cord until work measures 24 inches. BO all sts.

Button Loop

Using double-pointed needles and one strand each of MC and CC held together, work 4-st I-Cord until work measures 4 inches. BO all sts.

Finishing Instructions

Note: When sewing pouch, strap, and button loop, use yarn needle and a doubled strand of yarn.

Fold one short end of bag towards center of work, creating a pouch which is 12 inches deep and leaving a 6-inch flap. Sew side edges of pouch.

Sew ends of strap to side edges of bag.

Sew button loop in place at center of flap.

Full by hand or in the washing machine as directed in chapter 4.

Lay flat and allow to dry completely.

Use sewing needle and thread to sew button to bag, opposite button loop.

Variation

This pattern uses a few key elements of knit design for fulling. Remember how you work increases at one end and decreases at the other? That helps to prevent the cast on and cast off edges from flaring outward. The I-Cord, or "idiot cord" as it's sometimes called, is a common and simple way to create straps, cords, closures and other details. Other than that, the whole project is just a simple rectangle sewn in place before felting.

Use these principles to invent your own bag designs! Make a rectangle twice as long, and you'll have a book-sized bag instead of a casual pouch. Or, knit a second, smaller rectangle and sew in place to make a pocket on the outside of the bag. Using double-stranded yarn makes for quick knitting!

I'm On the Case

by Roxane Cerda

Never fails—you think "No problem, I can make a quick run to the store without lugging an 8-ton diaper bag," when half-way through the errand your baby makes "that" face. Compact and cute, whip up this felted case made to hold just one diaper and one small disposable packet of wipes, just in case.

Project Rating: Summer Fling

Cost: $25

Necessary Skills: knitting and purling (page 192); knitted cast on (page 191); fulling in the machine (page 50); needle felting on a flat surface (page 47)

Finished Size

One size:
Height: 10.5 inches
Width: 6 inches

Materials

- Cascade 220 (100g, 220 yd/201m, 100 percent Peruvian highland wool); color: Brown #7822; 2 skeins
- Substitution: Approx. 440 yd/402m worsted weight feltable wool. Ball band should indicate a stockinette st gauge of approx. 20 sts = 4 inches.
- US #7/4.5 mm knitting needles
- Approx. 0.5 ounce assorted dyed wool roving (I used various pinks)
- Scissors
- Needle felting supplies (see page 44)
- Sewing needle
- Sewing thread in color to match yarn
- Tapestry needle
- One large button
- 12 inches narrow elastic cord

Gauge

Approx. 20 sts = 4 inches/10cm in stockinette st

Pattern Note

Though fulled projects are usually worked on needles larger than those indicated on the yarn's ball band, this project is worked on the size of needles normally used for this yarn. Because the resulting knitted fabric is already fairly dense, it will take longer to full than a more loosely knit fabric, but the resulting piece will be very dense and firm.

Instructions

CO 94 sts.

Work in stockinette st until work measures 8.5 inches, ending with a RS row.

Next Row [WS]: BO 32 sts, p to end. 62 sts remain.

Next Row [RS]: P to end, CO 32 sts. 94 sts.

Work in stockinette st until work measures 17 inches. BO all sts.

Finishing Instructions

Weave in ends.

Full in the washing machine as directed in Chapter 4.

Lay flat and pin to shape, so that piece measures approx. 12.5 inches by 17 inches.

Allow to dry completely.

Carefully trim the outer edges of the piece, so that it measures 12 inches by 16.5 inches. Do not trim the edges of the center split.

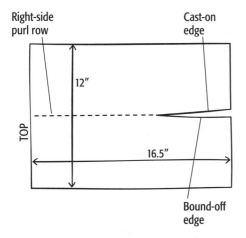

Place the felted piece, wrong side down, on the block of felting foam. Use the felting needle and pieces of colored roving to needle felt a design of your choice onto the body and flaps of the case. Directions for needle felting can be found in chapter 3.

Use sewing needle and thread to sew the edges of the fabric together along the center split. (The slightly rolled edges of the fabric along this split will enable the case to fold correctly.)

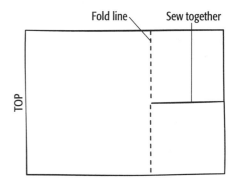

Fold fabric so that the section with the seamed center split forms a bisected pocket. Sew the outside edges of the pocket, then sew the center of the pocket, along the center seam, to the back of the case.

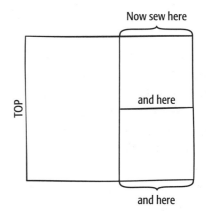

Thread the elastic cord onto the tapestry needle. Insert the needle through the edge of the case, just above the top edge of

the pocket, from the inside to the outside of the fabric. Pull the elastic through the fabric until approx. 2 inches remain on the inside of the fabric, then draw the needle back through the fabric, very close to the first hole made by the needle.

Remove needle from elastic and adjust elastic so that ends are even, with approx. the last 2 inches of each end protruding on the inside of the case. Thread one of these ends through the button, and tie ends into a knot.

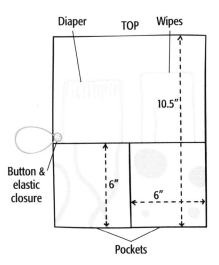

Variation

Okay, if you're not a mommy, an auntie, or a close friend of mommies, the diaper case is probably not up your alley. If you are a girly, though, this case will be. Even for mommies, it's nice to have a little, inconspicuous place to hide your–uh–feminine products. Follow the steps here to whip up a smaller version of the felted case to stash your tampons.

Because of the silk content of the yarn, your finished felt fabric will look a bit "crunchier" than a 100 percent wool fabric. This is a cool effect–feel free to play! Remember, when fulling a new-to-you yarn, you probably will want to whip up a test swatch ahead of time.

Project Rating: Summer Fling
Cost: $15
Necessary Skills: Same as I'm On the Case

Finished Size
Height: 6.5 inches
Width: 4 inches

Materials

- Jo Sharp Silk Road DK Tweed (50g (1 3/4 oz), 147 yd/135m, 85 percent wool, 10 percent silk, and 5 percent cashmere), color: Magnolia #407; 1 ball
- Substitution: Approx. 147 yd/135m worsted weight feltable wool blend. Ball band should indicate a stockinette st gauge of approx. 20 sts = 4 inches.
- US #7/4.5mm knitting needles
- Approx. 0.25 ounce assorted dyed roving (I used various pinks)
- Scissors
- Needle felting supplies (see page 44)
- Sewing needle
- Sewing thread in color to match your yarn
- Tapestry needle
- Two snaps

Gauge

Approx. 20 sts = 4 inches/10cm in stockinette st

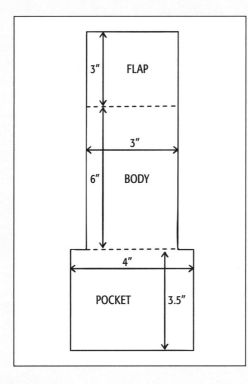

Finishing Instructions

Weave in ends.

Full in the washing machine as directed in chapter 4. Lay flat and allow to dry completely.

Needle felt as in main pattern.

Fold the longer, wider end of the piece along the purl ridge to form a pocket. Use sewing thread and needle to sew edges of pocket. Sew snaps onto case as shown.

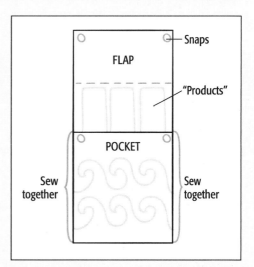

Instructions

CO 20 sts.
Work 30 rows in stockinette st, ending with a WS row.
Next Row [RS]: P all sts.
Work 60 rows in stockinette st.
Next Row [WS]: K all sts.
Next Row [RS]: [K5, m1] 3 times, k5. 23 sts.
Work 37 rows in stockinette st. BO all sts.

Ah! Savasana! Yoga Mat Bag

This stunner happily totes your yoga mat to and from practice without losing that zen feeling. Knit modularly in a self-striping yarn, the colors blend casually from square to square. After felting, the exact size can be altered slightly to provide a cutom fit for your mat! The technique shown here, I like to call *patchwork knitting*. If you flip ahead a few chapters, you'll see how designer Belinda Fireman adapted the technique into the spectacular Rainbow Bridge Baby Blanket on page 164. Patchwork knitting is really well suited for fulling. Because you're knitting each square concentrically, it's possible to obtain true squares after fulling, and therefore, is a great tool for design.

Project Rating: Love 'o Your Life

Cost: $100–$120

Necessary Skills: basic knitting (page 191); single crochet (page 187); fulling in the machine (page 50); knitting in the round (page 193); picking up stitches (page 194)

Techniques:

K2tog Knit next two stitches together

SKP Slip 1 st, knit next st, pass slipped stitch over stitch just knit (as if binding off).

Finished Size

Fits an average yoga mat. Exact size can be controlled during the fulling process.

Materials

- Noro Kureyon (50g, 109 yd/100m, 100 percent wool), color: #148; 15 balls
- Substitution: Approx. 1639 yd/1500m worsted weight feltable wool. Ball band will indicate a gauge of approx. 18 inches = 4 inches in stockinette st.
- 1 set of five US 10/6mm double-pointed needles
- 1 US J/10 / 6mm crochet hook
- Yarn needle
- Non-separating, heavy-duty zipper, 36 inches long
- Sewing needle
- Sewing thread to match prevalent color of yarn
- Stitch markers

Gauge

Gauge isn't important for this pattern. Just be sure to use a large enough needle to obtain a loosely knit fabric.

Pattern Notes

To make this bag, you'll be knitting a series of squares to create a rectangle composed of 7 by 11 *square motifs*. As promised, the pattern requires absolutely no seaming (except for sewing in the zipper). After the first square is worked, the remaining squares will be attached by picking up some stitches, and casting on others. The strap is a long strip of 21 square motifs.

This allows for quite a bit of flexibility. Do you need some portability in your knitting? Instead of working on a single large

Top: The Ultra-Simple One Night Bag (see page 82) and Bottom: Ah! Savasana! Handbag (variation of Ah! Savasana! Yoga Mat Bag; see page 91)

I'm On the Case (see page 84)

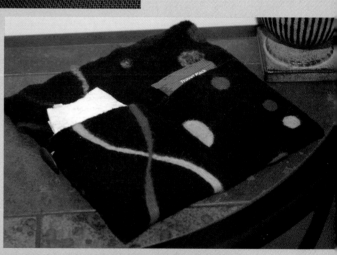

Case lying open

Variation of I'm On the Case; see page 86

Ah! Savasana! Yoga Mat Bag (see page 88)

Wrapped and ready to give

Opened

Some Assembly Required (see page 92)

Ready to assemble

Holy Smokes! (A Holey Tote) (see page 95)

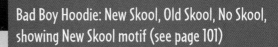

Bad Boy Hoodie: New Skool, Old Skool, No Skool, showing New Skool motif (see page 101)

Bad Boy Hoodie: New Skool, Old Skool, No Skool, showing Old Skool and No Skool motifs (see page 101)

Menswear for You (see page 105)

Cropped Cardigan, front (see page 107)

Cropped Cardigan, back (see page 107)

Slocks and Slocks variation (see page 109)

Don't Give the Mittens (see page 112)

Loopy Boa
(see page 123)

"Junior" Varsity Jacket
(see page 118)

Variation on Loopy Boa (see page 124)

Sideways Striped Scarf (see page 125) and Scarf for the Subzero Urban Dweller (see page 129)

Wild Thing Scarf (see page 127)

Featherweight Scarf (see page 131)

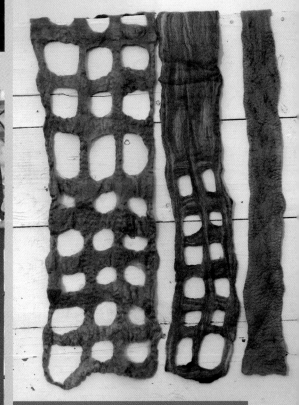

From left to right, two variations on Featherweight Scarf (see page 132) and variation on Sideways Striped Scarf (see page 126)

Swing Raglan (see page 133)

The Save-Your-Marriage Knitting Needle Roundup (see page 137)

Inside of needle case

Spring Is Sprung (see page 141)

Flower variation of Spring Is Sprung (see page 141)

Skull variation of Spring Is Sprung (see page 142)

Chunky Bead Necklace (see page 143)

Fishin' for Kittens Toy (see page 145)

Uber Chunky Felted Yarn (see page 147)

Moleskine Jacket (see page 149)

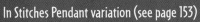
In Stitches Pendant variation (see page 153)

In Stitches Earrings (see page 151)

Felted Soapy Blue Balls (see page 157)
and Get Off Your Felted Soap Box
(see page 159)

Who Needs Flowers? Vases for Crafters (see page 162)

Rainbow Bridge Baby Blanket
(see page 164)

Octopillow (see page 169)

Hoodie variation of Octopillow (see page 170)

sheet of squares, make two smaller 7 by 5 rectangles and attach them together with a row of squares down the middle.

Start with the first square and then work as you like. It can be fun to shake up the colors a bit by jumping around instead of placing each new square next to the previous square. But, I'll leave that up to you!

Square Motif

Divide 48 sts equally between 4 double-pointed needles and join to begin working in the round, being careful not to twist.

Odd-numbered Rounds 1–9: K all sts.

Round 2: [K2tog, k8, SKP] 4 times. 40 sts remain.

Round 4: [K2tog, k6, SKP] 4 times. 32 sts remain.

Round 6: [K2tog, k4, SKP] 4 times. 24 sts remain.

Round 8: [K2tog, k2, SKP] 4 times. 16 sts remain.

Round 10: [K2tog, SKP] 4 times. 8 sts remain.

Break yarn, draw through remaining sts and pull tight.

Instructions

First Square

Using double-pointed needles, CO 48 sts. Work Square Motif.

Square Attached On One Side

Using double-pointed needles, CO 36 sts. Continuing from these sts, pick up and k 12 sts along one edge of a bordering square. Work Square Motif.

Square Attached on Two Adjacent Sides

Using double-pointed needles, CO 24 sts. Continuing from these sts, pick up and k 12 sts along an edge of one square, and 12 sts along the edge of a diagonally adjacent square. Work Square Motif.

Square Attached on Two Opposite Sides

Using double-pointed needles, CO 12 sts. Continuing from these sts, pick up and k 12 sts along an edge of one square; CO 12 more sts, then pick up and k 12 sts along an edge of another square. Work Square Motif.

Square Attached on Three Sides

Using double-pointed needles, CO 24 sts. Continuing from these sts, pick up and k 12 sts along an edge of one square, 12 sts along an edge of a diagonally adjacent square, and 12 sts along an edge of a third diagonally adjacent square. Work Square Motif.

Bag Instructions

Work squares as above until you have formed a rectangle which is 11 squares long and 7 squares wide.

When all squares are complete, work end of bag as follows:

Bag End

Using double-pointed needles, pick up and k 12 sts along the edge of each square along one short end of the bag, placing a st marker after each 12 sts. 84 sts.

Divide sts between needles, place marker and join to begin working in the round.

Round 1: K all sts.

Round 2: [K to 2 sts before marker, k2tog] 7 times.

Repeat these 2 rounds 6 times more. 35 sts.

Work Round 2 three times. 14 sts.

Break yarn, draw through remaining sts and pull tight.

Edging

Along the long edges of the rectangle (which will form the side opening of the bag), work 1 row of single crochet, working 1 sc for every 2 sts. This will help prevent these edges from flaring too much during fulling.

Strap

At lower edge of bag, locate square opposite opening (there will be 3 squares on either side of this square). Work Square Attached On One Side, attaching to lower edge of this square.

Continue working squares, attaching each to the top edge of the previous square, until you have worked 21 squares.

If the strap looks excessively long, it's because this strap is used to tie the top end of the bag closed. It's possible to cut off any excess fabric after fulling. So, you'll want to err on the side of excess instead of skimping here. I know you're probably sick to death of squares, but persevere a little longer! It's worth it!

Finishing Instructions

Use yarn needle to loosely secure all ends, to prevent unraveling in the wash.

Full as directed in Chapter 4, checking the size occasionally to ensure a proper fit.

When the bag has shrunk to the desired shape, size, and density, stretch and pull to block into shape. Lay flat and allow to dry completely.

Sew zipper into bag opening.

Insert your yoga mat into the side of the bag. Take the strap and tie it securely around the open end of the bag, leaving plenty of room to get the mat in and out. You'll probably want to try zipping the bag up, to make sure you can fully close the bag without the strap getting in the way.

This is the time to adjust the length of your strap, if desired. Be sure to leave enough length in the strap for the bag to sling comfortably over your shoulder. Once you are satisfied, cut away any excess.

Use a sewing needle and thread to secure the knotted strap to the top of the bag.

Variation

Not into yoga? Use the same guidelines to knit a cute handbag. Try a rectangle 5 squares wide and 7 squares long, to make a 13 by 8 inch purse. Of course, you'll need a lot less yarn! For a bag of this size, try approx. 400m of yarn. Alternately, try the purse photographed. It's also made from Noro Kureyon, it has 20 squares arranged in a 4 by 5 rectangle. The only real change to the pattern above? We knit two bag ends, each over 60 sts instead of 84 sts (again, 12 sts were picked up in each square).

This technique is flexible and fun to adapt to just about anything. Don't miss Belinda Fireman's Rainbow Bridge Baby Blanket in chapter 9 for a great example!

Some Assembly Required

by Cecily Keim

You can never have two many sweet, colorful little wallets or purses. Share the magic of fulling with a friend! Start the project, and hand the rest off in a gift kit. After all, it would be selfish to keep all the fun for yourself!

Project Rating: Flirtation

Cost: $20

Necessary Skills: ch (page 186); sc (page 187); sl st (page 187); sewing ends (page 194); whip stitch; fulling in the machine (page 50)

Finished Size:

Width: 4.5 inches

Height when closed: 3 inches

Materials

- Blue Sky Alpacas Sport Weight 100 percent baby alpaca (50g, 110 yd/100m, baby alpaca); less than 1 skein each color
- [MC] Color: #531 Paprika
- [CC] Color: #520 Avocado
- Substitution: Sport weight, feltable alpaca or wool yarn; approx. 30 yd/27.5m of MC and only a few yards/meters of CC for each circle are required.
- US K / 6.5mm crochet hook
- US G7 / 4.5mm crochet hook
- Sharp yarn needle
- Small pieces of hook and loop tape (Velcro)
- Sewing thread in colors to both match and contrast with wallet body
- Sewing needle
- Buttons, sequins, beads, etc.

Gauge

Approx. 12 sc = 4 inches on 6.5 mm hook

Pattern Notes

Working into Front or Back Loop: When crocheting the wallet, you will be instructed to work into the front or back loop of a stitch. This refers to the two loops of the chain-like formation which forms the top of a crochet stitch. The front loop refers to the loop of this chain which is closest to you, and the back loop refers to the loop which is furthest.

Instructions

Wallet

Using larger hook and MC, ch 20.

Row 1: Sc in second ch from hook and in each ch to end. 19 sc.

Row 2: Ch 1; working into back loops only, sc in each sc to end.

Row 3: Ch 1; working into front loops only, sc in each sc to end.

Repeat Rows 2 and 3 eighteen times more, then work Row 2 once more. 40 rows have been worked. Break yarn, draw through loop and pull tight.

Weave in ends.

Circle (Make as many as desired)

Using smaller hook and CC, ch 2.

Round 1: Work 6 sc in second ch from hook, sl st in first sc to join into a circle.

Round 2: Ch 1, 2 sc in first sc and in each sc to end, sl st in first sc. 12 sc.

Round 3: Ch 1, [2 sc in first sc, 1 sc in next sc] to end, sl st in first sc. 18 sc.

Break yarn, draw through loop and pull tight.

Weave in ends.

Finishing Instructions

Fulling

Place wallet and circle(s) into mesh bag and full according to directions in Chapter 4, checking progress frequently (approx. every 3 minutes). If the recommended yarn is used, the pieces may develop a curly, boucle-like texture while fulling. If you wish to maintain this texture, stop fulling before the curls are completely matted down.

When desired size and density are achieved, remove pieces from washing machine. Use your fingers to mold wallet body into an even rectangle. Fold wallet body approximately in thirds, so that when seamed along the sides it will form a small pouch with an overlapping flap (see color insert photo). Place a folded paper towel inside wallet, lay circles and folded wallet on a towel and allow to dry completely.

Assembly

Before seaming, determine desired location of velcro closure. Use sewing needle and thread that matches wallet body in order to sew velcro pieces to wallet body and flap.

Use MC and yarn needle to sew sides of wallet, leaving flap free. The whip stitch is recommended for sewing these seams.

Decorating

Arrange circles as desired and sew in place using CC. Gather your buttons, beads, and any other embellishments you might like to use, along with a few different contrasting colors of sewing thread. Place them on the wallet and flap, experimenting with different arrangements until you find one you like. Sew the embellishments securely to the wallet and enjoy!

Variation

The buttons used to embellish this wallet can be used as functional closures, too! To incorporate buttonholes, do the following:

Work the Wallet pattern as written until 37 rows have been worked.
Next Row: Ch 1; working into both loops, sc in first five sc, ch 4, skip next 2 sc, sc in next sc, ch 6, skip next 3 sc, sc in next sc, ch 4, skip next 2 sc, sc in last 5 sc.
Break yarn, draw through loop and pull tight.
Weave in ends. Follow finishing directions as above.

The elements of this project make a great gift kit! Place the following in a small box and wrap attractively:

- ◆ Unfelted wallet body and a circle or three
- ◆ A handwritten card with instructions for felting and decorating
- ◆ Hook and loop tape, sewing thread and needle
- ◆ Yarn for seaming and sharp yarn needle
- ◆ Buttons, beads, etc.

Holy Smokes! (A Holey Tote)

by Debora Lloyd

Debora is always trying to "make room for spirit" in her life, so she likes to knit around space as part of her designs. At first she was satisfied with lace knitting, but with the discovery of felted fabric the spaces are getting larger and more numerous. This intermediate bag is really just full of evenly spaced, very large, one-row buttonholes. Before felting, the purse looks like a Halloween mask for a multi-eyed alien.

Project Rating: Summer Fling

Cost: $40–$60, depending largely on fabric choice

Necessary Skills: fulling in the machine (page 50); basic knitting (page 191); I-Cord (page 82)

Finished Size

Width: 15 inches
Depth: 13 inches

Materials

- Malabrigo merino worsted (100 grams, 215 yd/196m; 100% merino wool); color #204 Velvet Grapes; 3 skeins
- Substitution: Approx. 645 yd/588m aran weight feltable wool
- 1 set US #11/8mm straight needles
- Two US #11/8mm double-pointed needles
- 0.5 yd fabric for lining–be sure to choose a reversible fabric!
- Sharp yarn needle
- Sewing needle
- Sewing thread
- 1 large snap fastener

Gauge

Approx. 14 sts = 4 inches in garter stitch
Gauge is not important for this project; just be sure to obtain a loosely knit fabric.

Pattern Notes

Work 7-st Buttonhole: Slip next 2 sts to right needle, pass first slipped st over second slipped st and off needle, (slip next st to right needle, pass previous slipped st over last slipped st and off needle) 6 times, slip last slipped st back to left needle; turn work so that WS is facing, CO 7 sts using Knitted Cast On; turn work so that RS is facing, continue to work row.

Work 2-st Buttonhole: Slip next 2 sts to right needle, pass first slipped st over second slipped st and off needle, slip next st to right needle, pass previous slipped st over last slipped st and off needle, slip last slipped st back to left needle; turn work so that WS is facing, CO 2 sts using Knitted Cast On; turn work so that RS is facing, continue to work row.

Knitted Cast On: *Knit next stitch on left needle, but do not drop stitch from left needle; slip newly made st onto left needle.* Repeat from * to * for each st to be cast on.

I-Cord:

Using a double-point needle, CO required number of sts.

Next Row: Instead of turning work around to work back on the WS, slide all sts to other end of needle, switch needle back to your left hand, bring yarn around back of work, and start knitting the sts again. I-Cord is worked with the RS facing at all times.

Repeat this row to form I-Cord. After a few rows, work will begin to form a tube.

Buttonhole Pattern (Worked over a multiple of 10 sts + 3):

Rows 1–6: K all sts.

Row 7 [RS]: [K3, work 7-st buttonhole] 7 times, k3.

Rows 8–14: K all sts.

Row 15 [RS]: K8, [work 7-st buttonhole, k3] 6 times, k5.

Row 16 [WS]: K all sts.

Repeat Rows 1–16 for Buttonhole Pattern.

Instructions

Front

Using straight needles, CO 73 sts.

Work Rows 1–16 of Buttonhole Pattern three times, then work Rows 1–14 once more.

Note: Until you are comfortable with the Buttonhole Pattern, it may be useful to count your sts after Rows 7 and 15 of the pattern. You should always end up with 73 sts; if you have more or fewer sts, you may have bound off or cast on too many sts when working one of the buttonholes.

Bottom

Rows 1–4: K all sts.

Rows 5, 7, 9 [RS]: Ssk, ssk, k to last 4 sts, k2tog, k2tog. 61 sts remain when Row 9 is complete.

Rows 6, 8 [WS]: K all sts.

Row 10 [WS]: P all sts. This row marks the center bottom of the bag.

Rows 11, 13, 15 [RS]: [K1, m1] twice, k to last 2 sts, [m1, k1] twice. 73 sts when Row 15 is completed.

Rows 12, 14, 16 [WS]: K all sts.

Rows 17–20: K all sts.

Back

Work Rows 1–16 of Buttonhole Pattern three times, then work Rows 1–14 once more.

BO all sts.

Bands (Make Two)

sing 2 strands of yarn held together, CO 58 sts.

7 rows.

ext Row: K5, work 2-st buttonhole, k44, work 2-st buttonhole, k5.

4 rows. BO all sts.

Strap

sing a double-pointed needle and 2 strands of yarn held together, CO 3 sts.

ork I-Cord until work measures 65 inches. BO all sts.

Fulling

ull pieces according to directions in chapter 4, until pieces measure as follows:

Body: 16 by 23 inches
Bands: 2 by 16 inches
Strap: 52 inches long
Note: The bands may need to be fulled for longer than the strap and bag body, as the denser fabric will not full as easily.

Finishing Instructions

old bag body in half and sew side edges, beginning at fold and ending approx. 10 inches from fold.

lace bands inside upper edge of bag, so that the bag edges overlap them by approx. 0.5 inch. Sew in place.

Lining

old lining in half, with selvadge edges together. Lay bag on top of fabric, aligning bottom fold of bag with fold of fabric. Trace side edges of bag, marking fabric to indicate bottoms of bands and placement of side openings. Remove bag. Bag is lined only to lower edges of bands; draw a line to connect the marks on each side which indicate lower edges of bands. Trace a half-inch seam allowance around all edges. Cut out lining.

his is where you can really customize your bag by putting pockets on the inside. I usually put in a 1.5 inch-wide diagonal holder for my knitting needles, if I think I will use a bag for toting my knitting projects. You can even embroider your name, initials or special messages to the inside pockets before you sew up the sides of the lining.

ew side edges of lining, from fold to marks indicating side openings, leaving a half-inch seam allowance. Fold over the upper 0.5 inch of the lining and press.

lip lining into bag and sew neatly in place along all edges.

sing picture as a guide, thread strap through holes in bands. Trim to desired length and sew ends together. Sew snap halves inside bands, at center of bag opening.

Variation

Sewing skills not up to snuff? Knit your own bag lining by working a second rectangle in simple stockinette. Use yarn and a darning needle to sew in place before fulling. Full, and you have a self-lined bag. Don't forget to get creative with color. For the maximum amount of pizzazz, choose a contrasting color for the lining.

Chapter Seven

◆

Stuff to Wear

Bad Boy Hoodie: New Skool, Old Skool, No Skool

Needle felt these bad boy motifs onto your guy's favorite hoodie.

Menswear for You

Shrink a too-big sweater into a preppy vest.

Cropped Cardigan

A failed knitting project gets new life as a cropped fashion statement.

Slocks

Are they slippers? Are they chunky socks? In any case, these slocks will keep your tootsies warm and cozy all winter long.

Don't Give the Mittens

Learn Fair Isle stranded knitting on these chunky mittens! Any mistakes will be fulled away.

"Junior" Varsity Jacket

Dress your toddler for the big game in this varsity-inspired jacket.

Loopy Boa

The easiest of crochet combined with colorful yarn fulls into a loopy textured scarf.

Sideways Striped Scarf

Play with color and wet felting in this scarf project.

Wild Thing Scarf

Sew wool yarn onto a length of fabric for a dramatic wrap.

Scarf for the Subzero Urban Dweller

A great first wet felting project, this silk chiffon base has wool fiber felted on. Ultra-luxe, ultra-warm.

Featherweight Scarf

Super thin layers of fine fiber are wet felted together for a skinny scarf.

Swing Raglan

Felters can sew too! A basic raglan jacket sewing pattern is used with sheets of your own felted wool.

Bad Boy Hoodie: New Skool, Old Skool, No Skool

by Karen Harper

If you live in a house like mine where music comes from all sides (the man likes 80's break dancing and disco, the boy thinks Green Day IS old school and I am still mourning the loss of Joey Ramone) you need to find a good way to balance everything. This hoodie can show off your new school, old school or no school attitude. Wear it with pride and feel free to change it up.

Project Rating: Summer Fling

Cost: $10 plus cost of hoodie. We snagged this one at Old Navy for under $30.

Necessary Skills: Needle felting on a flat surface (page 47)

Finished Size

Main design on back about 10 inches by 8 (ish) inches
Front piece about 4 inches by 4 inches
Arm piece about 4 inches by 4 inches

Materials

- Black (or any color really) hoodie. Make sure it has been washed at least once! 100 percent cotton is best, but this can be done on cotton/acrylic blends successfully as well. (You could do these on a jean jacket if that's more your style)
- Pink roving or fleece, approx. 2 oz
- Blue roving or fleece, approx. 1 oz
- White roving or fleece, 1 oz
- Tiny pinch of orange or yellow roving or fleece for swallow's beak
- Red single ply wool yarn for Anarchy symbol, 5 yd or so
- Magenta and black wool yarn for outlines and skull teeth, about 10 yd
- 3 to 4 felting needles, size 38 star
- White chalk for tracing the templates
- Foam for needle felting, approximately 12 inches square and 2 inches thick

Templates

We've provided some designs for you to enlarge to the size you desire. You can use these as templates by using white chalk to transfer the designs to the hoodie (see the instructions that follow).

Instructions

After photocopying the design to the size you desire, trace on the top of the template with the chalk. Flip the template over and press it onto the hoodie in the desired location. The chalk will transfer the design onto the hoodie. Remember, this will reverse the design. If you're particular about the direction of the design, you can instead trace with chalk on the back of the photocopy. To do this, you may need to go over the template with a thick black marker first, so you can see the full design clearly.

Place the foam inside the hoodie so that it is under the area with the transferred design on it. Now you are ready to begin needle felting.

New Skool Skull

See the template for skull design. Follow the above instructions, remembering to enlarge or reduce the template to your desired size. Also remember to place the foam inside the hoodie under the area you intend to needle felt.

You'll want to start needle felting the main portion of the skull first. Always do the biggest area to begin. Lay down some pink roving inside the skull outlines from the center out and needle felt it onto your fabric. You can use one needle at a time if you are just starting out, but I recommend using two to three (or four if you are getting the hang of this) held in your hand to make the area being felted bigger. As shown in chapter 3, you can also buy a needle holder that enables you to work with three or more needles spaced further apart. The drawback to these tools? They're not as effective on small detailed areas. Experiment and work to your comfort level.

Work from the center of the skull outwards, leaving the eye, nose, and teeth areas empty, and needle felt the rest of the skull. Remember to move your piece around to ensure its being felted evenly. Nice job! You can tweak this as much as you want to.

Now turn your hoodie inside out. You should see almost the same thing in reverse on the inside of the fabric. You want to make sure there are lots of little fibers poked through. This is how you know you are making sure the fibers are uniform and becoming one integrated piece of fabric. If you see some blank spots, go over it from the right side to ensure its uniformity.

To create the outlines, place your wool yarn in position and needle felt it in place. You'll want to go around the outside of the skull, the eye and noe holes. Black yarn can also be used to create teeth, as shown.

Old Skool Swallows

Follow the above instructions using the swallow design. It's your choice as to which of the two swallows you needle felt — or maybe you'll want to do both of them! Remember to enlarge or reduce the template to your desired size and to place the foam inside the hoodie under the area you intend to needle felt.

Using your desired color of roving (in my case, blue), start needle felting on the top of swallow's back, moving out to his wings. You will then want to do the front and back parts of his little belly in white. Don't worry about doing the details yet; you'll get to them with your outlining. Fill in the big colored places first, and then add the smaller ones like the beak. Make sure to check that the wool is showing through to the inside of the fabric, as for the skull area above.

Finish off by outlining and doing your detail work, such as the little guy's feathers and eye, with your black wool.

No Skool Anarchy Symbol

Following the instructions above, use the template provided (reversing it if necessary), to transfer the pattern onto the hoodie. Remember to enlarge or reduce the template to your desired size and to place the foam inside the hoodie under the area you intend to needle felt.

Using the red single-ply wool, start with your circle and work in. Outline if desired.

Finishing Instructions

The most important thing about this project is making sure your needle felting is as flat and flush against the fabric as can be. It should be hard to pinch any fibers off it, and should look uniform in appearance. Make sure it's like a painting and you can't really see the fabric underneath it. You are looking for a nice smooth finish with no huge bumps.

our hoodie can be washed and dried in the machine, but make sure to turn it inside out first. You may need to refelt any loose pieces that come up and if it is in heavy use some pilling may happen. Just go over it again with the felting needle, and soon it will be one uniform piece of fabric.

Variation

Not Your Granny's Treasures

Wouldn't the swallows be lovely on a set of tea towels? Needle felt them in a friend's favorite colors to make a thoughtful housewarming gift. If flaming skulls rather than swallows are your thing, here's another template. You could put the pyro skull on the back of a hoodie or sweatshirt and the plain skull on the front. Or, create your own designs. It's as simple as tracing over a design from a stencil set, fabric, coloring book, or just about anything.

Menswear for You

In the past few years, the process of recycling old or ill-fitting sweaters by fulling in the washing machine has been all the rage. You've likely seen instructions for making purses, pillows, throw blankets, and more. But, the sturdy and soft felt that you can create is also well-suited to garments. This men's Fair Isle pullover never fit me properly. It was too wide, too short, too baggy, too unflattering. Determined to make it work, I fulled the sweater and cut it into a snazzy and fashionable vest. Two words of advice: *buy big.* And, be prepared to run into a couple of failed experiments along the way. Worst-case scenario? Anything that shrinks too much, you can easily sew into a throw pillow or set aside for making patchwork bags, such as the fab Save Your Marriage Needle Case in chapter 8. The best part about these projects? You can feel like a fashion designer, even if you've never knit or sewn a stitch in your life. Just cut away!

Project Rating: Flirtation to Love o' Your Life, depending on embellishments

Cost: Free to $20, depending on your thrift-store scavenger abilities

Necessary Skills: Fulling in the machine (page 50); sewing (optional)

Finished Size

Shrink it as much as you'd like . . . with this project, the finished size is up to you!

Materials

- 1 man's pullover, much larger than your actual measurements. (I used a Peruvian wool Fair Isle, approx. 48 inches in circumference and 12 inches from underarms, 20 inches from shoulders.)
- Washing machine for fulling
- Lingerie bag to fit, old sheets, tennis balls or other fulling supplies (see chapter 4)
- Scissors

Instructions

Full the sweater in the machine to the desired fabric and/or size. Check out chapter 4 for details! The size is most important at this point. However, since you won't be finishing the edges, the fabric should also be firm enough to prevent unraveling. You want the width of the sweater to be the correct width for your body. If it's too big and you can still see the individual stitches, keep on shrinking! This may take several passes through the washing machine.

Cut off the sleeves and neckband.

Put on the vest, while it's still wet, and stretch it to fit. If making the vest for a different sized person, you'll want to pull and prod the fabric with your hands until it measures the proper size for that person. When in doubt, guess on the larger side!

After your vest is stretched to fit, take it off and let it dry flat on towels or on a sweater rack. After it's dry, use the scissors to cut out a different neckline or shoulders to fit. When in doubt, use a favorite tank or tee to "stencil" the right shape.

Optional Finishing Instructions

Are you a whiz at the sewing machine? Consider machine-stitching around the neck, hem, and arm openings for an unstructured look. Alternately, check out the variation that follows for embellishment ideas.

Variation

Embellishment Ideas

1 From a length of silk chiffon or gauze in a complementary color, cut out two rectangles approximately 6 inches wide and twice as long as half the length of the vest. In my case, each rectangle was 44 inches by 6 inches

2 On the rectangles, sew long stitches approximately ½ inch in from one long edge.

3 Fold and press at sewn edge. Sew another hem ¼ inches in from edge, catching the first hem. Repeat for other rectangle.

4 With right sides together, sew each 6-inch edge together to form side seams. Use a French hem if desired.

5 Working approximately ½ inch in from unhemmed edge, loosely baste around top of ruffle. Repeat approximately ¼ inch away from edge, working in a parallel line to the first basting stitches.

6 Using pins and fingers and working from both side seams, pull on both basting lines to form gathers.

7 Turn vest inside out and overlap ruffled chiffon with hem of vest as shown in the photos. Pin and sew in place.

8 Take lace, ribbon, or rick rack in coordinating color and sew in place along neck and arm holes.

Cropped Cardigan

If you're a knitter, you probably have a few unwearable sweaters languishing in the back of your closet. Maybe they're ill-fitting . . . too large in the arms, too wide in the body. Or maybe you have an unwanted gift. The color is good, but it's way too big. In this case, the cardigan was originally a turtleneck pullover, one of my first hand-knit sweaters. The yarn was an angora/wool blend that refused to stop leaving a hot-pink trail on every possible surface. Unwearable? Yes! But add a little hot water, and the angora felts into a smooth and shed-free surface. After fulling, the sweater is then cut into a smooth-front cardigan, and a series of grommets are added to the back to make a lace-up back and prevent flaring

Project Rating: Flirtation

Cost: Less than $15, if you already have a suitable sweater

Necessary Skills: Fulling in the machine (page 50)

Finished Size

As shown, the garment fits a 36–38 inch chest; however, the exact size is determined by the original garment proportions, as well as the amount of felting, fiber content, and so on.

We used a 42 inch finished measurement pullover.

Materials

- Shrinkable pullover sweater
- 8 8mm / $^5/_{16}$ inch silver grommets and grommet tool
- Measuring tape
- Good quality fabric scissors
- 1 yd of black ribbon, $^1/_4$ inches to $^1/_2$ inches wide

Instructions

Full the sweater to the desired size and fabric. For hints and tips, review the information in chapter 4.

While sweater is still wet, put it on and pull, prod, and stretch into the right shape. The bottom hem of the sweater will flare in the back. . . don't worry about this for now! We'll cut out a dart after the sweater is dry.

Remove sweater, lay flat, and carefully and very evenly cut a line up the front of the sweater to create the cardigan opening. If you can still see individual stitches, you can use this as a guide. Otherwise, you may want to measure and mark the line before cutting.

Lay flat or hang to dry.

Finishing Instructions

A friend comes in handy at this point! Put on the cardigan and decide how much extra fabric needs to be removed from the back. In most cases, you'll be looking at a 6-inches-high triangle, approximately 4 inches wide at the bottom.

First, cut a line straight up the center of the back of the cardigan, 6 inches long.

Next, use a measuring tape to measure 2 inches to the side of the cut you just made Cut evenly from here to the top of the initial cut. Repeat for the other side.

Now, add the grommets, four on either side of the triangle, or as desired, as directed on the package.

Lace up with ribbon until you have a good fit.

Variation

Not into ribbons and bows? Lace up the back with a series of lightweight silver chains instead. Or, use strips of black leather. The harder edge will contrast nicely with the fuzzy comfort of the felt.

A lot of the variations on a shrunken sweater depend on any fit problems. Are the sleeves too tight? Cut out a slash from the top of each sleeve to line up with your bicep. Add grommets here and lace up as well. Or, cut a slash from the cuff to the elbow instead.

Slocks

Are they slippers? Are they socks? They fit like socks but are cozy like slippers. So, some of my friends dubbed them "slocks"! Whatever you call them, they knit up in a flash and make great last minute gifts. To knit these, you'll need to be comfortable knitting and purling, as well as knitting in the round. This pattern uses a short row technique to shape the toe and heel. If it sounds weird, don't worry. It is a little weird. Just have patience and follow the pattern. It works, I promise!

Project Rating: Summer Fling

Cost: $20 for one pair

Necessary Skills: Basic knitting skills (page 191), fulling in the machine (page 50)

Finished Size

Fits S–M [M–L, L, XL] feet
Exact size can be adjusted during the fulling process

Materials

- Cascade 220 (100g, 220 yd/201m, 100 percent Peruvian highland wool); 1 skein each MC and CC

For Burgundy/Gold Speckled Slocks:
- MC: Color: 7825 (gold)
- CC1: Color: 9404 (burgundy)

For Pink/Gray Mismatched Slocks:
- MC: Color: 8400 (gray)
- CC1: Color: 9477 (pink)
- 1 set US 11/9mm double-pointed needles
- Yarn needle
- Stitch markers
- 2 plastic bags for blocking

Gauge

Exact gauge is unimportant. Just be sure the fabric is loosely knit.

Pattern Notes

Wrap & Turn [W&T]

To wrap and turn on a RS row: Knit to point specified in pattern, bring yarn to front of work between needles, slip next stitch to right-hand needle, bring yarn around this stitch to back of work, slip stitch back to left-hand needle, turn work to begin purling back in the other direction.

To wrap and turn on a WS row: Purl to point specified in pattern, bring yarn to back of work between needles, slip next stitch to right-hand needle, bring yarn around this stitch to front of work, slip stitch back to left-hand needle, turn work to begin knitting back in the other direction.

Working Wraps Together with Wrapped Stitches

When working rows which follow short rows: Work the "wraps" at the turning points of the short rows, together with the stitches they wrap, as follows:

When working a RS row: Knit to wrapped stitch. Slip next stitch from left needle to right needle, use tip of left needle to pick up "wrap" and place it on right needle, insert left needle into both wrap and stitch, and knit them together.

When working a WS row: Purl to wrapped stitch. Slip next stitch from left needle to right needle, use tip of left needle to pick up "wrap" and place it on right needle, slip both wrap and stitch back to left needle, purl together through back loops.

Instructions

Note: Instructions are provided for working slocks with a contrasting toe and heel, as photographed in pink and grey. Because you'll be working with a doubled strand of yarn, it helps to wind each skein into two separate balls before beginning to knit. To create the speckled Burgundy/Gold slocks, simply hold one strand of MC and one strand of CC together throughout.

Toe

Using two strands of MC held together, CO 18[18, 20] sts.

Row 1 (WS): P all sts.

Row 2 (RS): *K to last st, W&T.

Row 3 (WS): P to last st, W&T.

Row 4 (RS): K to st before last wrapped st, W&T.

Row 5 (WS): P to st before last wrapped st, W&T.

Repeat Rows 4 and 5, 4[4, 5] times more. 6[6, 7] sts are wrapped on each side of work; the 6 sts in the center of the work are unwrapped. You will be ready to start a RS row.

Note: Before proceeding, be sure to review the "Working Wraps Together with Wrapped Stitches" instructions earlier in this section.

When wrapping stitches at turning points of short rows which follow, note that stitches will now have two wraps; these stitches will be referred to as double-wrapped stitches. When working a double-wrapped stitch on a subsequent row, pick up both wraps and work them together with the stitch which had been wrapped.

Row 6 (RS): K to first wrapped st, k together with wrap as described above. W&T.

Row 7 (WS): P to first wrapped st, p together with wrap as described above, W&T.

Row 8 (RS): K to first double wrapped st, k together with wraps, W&T.

Row 9 (WS): P to first double wrapped st, p together with wraps, W&T.

Repeat Rows 8 and 9 4[4, 5] times more. All sts have been worked. Toe is complete; you will be ready to work a RS row.**

Foot

Note: Foot will be worked in the round.

Round 1: With a doubled strand of CC, K9 [9, 10] using first needle, k remaining 9[9, 10] sts using a second needle; use third needle to pick up and k 18 [18, 20] sts along CO edge of Toe. 36 [36, 40] sts.

Work in stockinette st (k every round) until slock measures 9[10, 11] inches from tip of toe, ending at the end of the second needle.

Heel

Work from * to ** as for Toe, using a doubled strand of MC, working over the 18[18, 20] sts on third needle only.

Next Round: Switch back to doubled strand of CC . K to end of third needle, pick up and k 3 sts in gap between third needle and first needle; k to end of first needle; k to end of second needle and pick up 3 sts in gap between second needle and third needle. 42[42, 46] sts.

K 1 round.

Next Round: K18[18, 20], k2tog, k20[20, 22], k2tog. 40[40, 44] sts.

K 1 round.

Next Round: [K18[18, 20], k2tog] twice. 38[38, 40] sts.

K 4 rounds. BO all sts loosely.

Finishing Instructions

Loosely weave any ends to prevent unraveling.

Full in the washing machine as directed in chapter 4. Remember to check the size often!

To achieve the correct size, the slocks will need to be fulled until the fabric is very firm. You are unlikely to end up with a slock that is too small; if anything, you should end up with one that is slightly too large. If this happens, just keep shrinking until you can no longer see individual stitches! Remember, yarn substitution can have an effect on the amount and rate of shrinkage when fulling. If in doubt, test a swatch ahead of time.

Once your slocks are the right size, place a plastic bag on each foot and put on your slocks! They will mold to the shape of your feet. After you've worn the pair for 15 or 20 minutes, remove and allow to dry completely.

Variation

The great thing about these slocks is that it's possible to knit one in an evening, making it a quick project that's good for experimentation! With two strands of yarn held together, you can have a lot of control over the appearance of your slocks. Try a double strand of the same color for a solid look. Or, consider kicky stripes.

Don't Give the Mittens

by Dana Codding

Mitten (to get or give the): A lady, in turning down a proposal, is said to have given the gentleman the mitten. I don't recommend giving these mittens away, as they're the warmest, softest mittens on the planet. Felting windproofs the fabric and wool insulates even when warm. Don these for commuting or snowball fights!

Project Rating: Summer Fling

Cost: $20

Necessary Skills: Knitting in the round on double-pointed needles (page 193); following a chart; stranded knitting with two colors; fulling in the machine (page 50)

Techniques:

K2tog Knit the next two stitches together as one

SSK Slip the next two stitches knitwise, one at a time, to the right needle. Insert the left needle from front to back through these two stitches and knit them together.

M1 Make one stitch by inserting the left needle, from front to back, under the horizontal strand of yarn between the stitch just knit and the next stitch, and knitting it through the back loop.

Backwards Loop Cast On Form a twisted loop of yarn in the color indicated by the chart, and place it on the right needle.

Three-Needle Bind Off Hold both layers of knitting with right sides together. *Insert needle into first st on front needle and first st on back needle, and knit them together. Repeat this for the next st on the front and back needles. Draw the first st worked over the second st.* Repeat from * to * until all sts have been bound off. Break yarn and draw through remaining st.

Finished Size

Child [Woman, Man]
Hand Circumference at Palm 7[8, 9] inches
Mitten Length 8[9.5, 11] inches

Materials

- Brown Sheep Lamb's Pride Worsted (4 oz, 190 yds /173m, 85 percent wool / 15 percent mohair), 1 ball each color
- MC: Color - #M-151 Chocolate Souffle
- CC: Color - #M-34 Victorian Pink
  Substitution: Approx. 100m each color; aran weight, feltable wool
- 1 set US 10.5 / 6.5mm double-pointed needles
- Yarn needle
- Approx. 1 yd of scrap yarn to hold the thumb stitches. For best results, select a smooth yarn in a contrasting color.

Gauge

14 sts / 16 rows = 4 inches

Note: Gauge is approximate. Felting is very forgiving—if your gauge is close, your mittens will turn out fine. You can also customize the fit by watching the felting process very closely and removing the mittens from the washing machine when they fit you perfectly!

Instructions

Note: See charts for child's, woman's, and man's mittens on pages 115, 116, and 117.

Right Mitten

Using MC, *CO 27[31, 35] sts. Divide between double-pointed needles, place marker and join to begin working in the round, being careful not to twist.

K 4 rounds.

Join CC and work rounds 1–16[20, 24] of Right Mitten chart for chosen size.*

Next Round (Round 17[21, 25]): K1 using CC, place next 8[10, 12] sts on hold on waste yarn, work to end of round according to chart.

Work remaining rounds of chart.

When all rounds of chart are complete, turn mitten inside out and join top of mitten using Three-Needle Bind Off.

Thumb

Place held sts on two double-pointed needles, rejoin MC and k all sts; using a third needle, pick up and k 1 st in space between sts just knit and sts cast on over thumb gusset, pick up and k 1 st in each cast on st, pick up and k 1 st in space. 16[18, 20] sts.

Next Round: K8[10, 12], k2tog, k4, k2tog. 14[16, 18] sts.

K 8[13, 18] rounds.

Shape top of thumb: [K2tog, k1] 11[11, 13] times. 3[5, 5] sts remain. Break yarn, draw through remaining sts and pull tight.

Left Mitten

Work from * to * as for Right Mitten, working from Left Mitten chart.

Next Round (Round 17[21, 25]): Work first 9[10, 13] sts of round according to chart, place next 8[10, 12] sts on hold on waste yarn, work to end of round according to chart.

Continue as for Right Mitten.

Finishing Instructions

Weave in ends.

Full according to directions in chapter 4, checking progress frequently to ensure a correct fit.

hen mittens are fulled, lay flat and allow to dry completely.

f mittens are too fuzzy after fulling, they can be trimmed with electric clippers or a safety razor.

Child's Mitten, Left

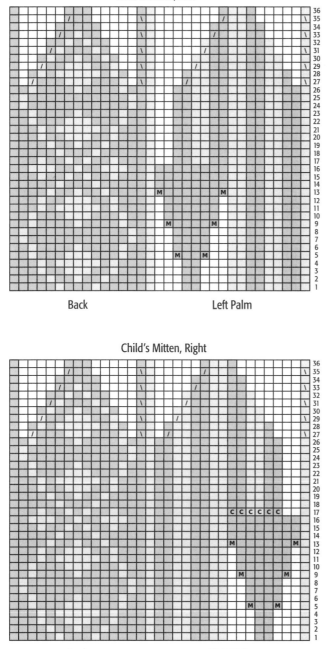

Back   Left Palm

Child's Mitten, Right

Back   Right Palm

M	Make 1
C	Cast on
/	K2tog
****	SSK
	No stitch (ignore this space)
	MC
	CC

Woman's Mitten, Left

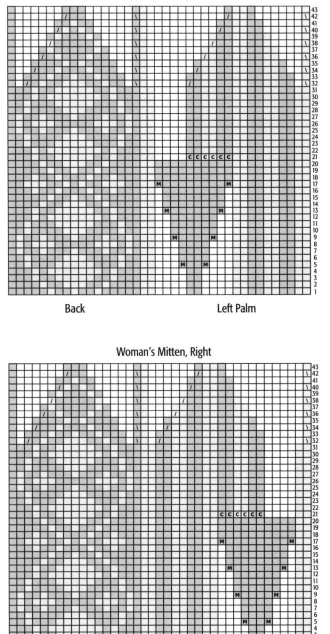

Back   Left Palm

Woman's Mitten, Right

Back   Right Palm

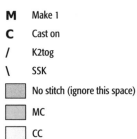

M	Make 1
C	Cast on
/	K2tog
****	SSK
▨	No stitch (ignore this space)
▨	MC
☐	CC

Man's Mitten, Left

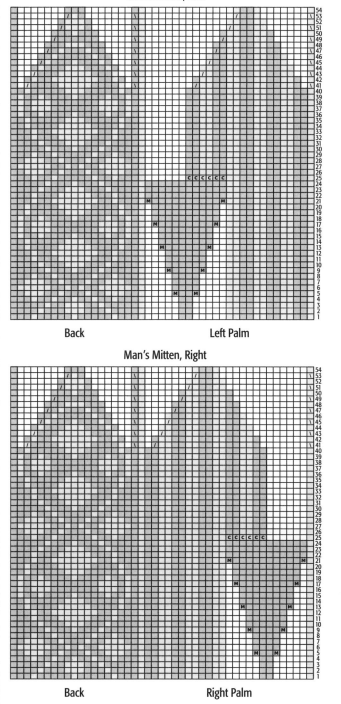

Back   Left Palm

Man's Mitten, Right

Back   Right Palm

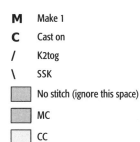

M — Make 1

C — Cast on

/ — K2tog

**** — SSK

No stitch (ignore this space)

MC

CC

"Junior" Varsity Jacket

by Amy O'Neill Houck

Remember that cozy varsity jacket you borrowed from your high school sweetheart? Now you can warm up your favorite toddler with this knitted and felted version. The combination of knitting, felting, and fun tools like a snap setter make this an adventurous and exciting project.

Project Rating: Love o' Your Life

Cost: $50

Necessary Skills: Basic knitting skills (see page 191); basic hand- or machine-sewing skills; fulling in the machine (page 50)

Techniques:

k2tog Knit the next two stitches together as one.

SSK Slip the next two stitches knitwise, one at a time, to the right needle. Insert the left needle from front to back through these two stitches and knit them together.

Finished Size

12m, 18m, 2T
Chest: 20[22, 24] inches
Back Length: 12.5[13, 13.5] inches

Materials

- MC: Cascade 220 Heathers (100g, 220 yd/ 201m, 100 percent wool), Color 2429; 4 skeins
- CCI: Cascade 220 Superwash (100g, 220 yd/ 201m, 100 percent wool), Color #875; 2 skeins
  Substitution: Approximately 900 yd of worsted weight wool are required for MC; approx. 300 yd

of superwash worsted weight wool are needed for CC. Ball band will indicate a gauge in stockinette st of approx. 20 sts = 4 inches.

- 1 pair US #8/5mm needles
- 1 pair US #9/5.5mm needles
- ½ yrd cotton ribbing
- 6-8 heavy duty snaps and snap setter (be sure to have 1–2 snaps more than you wish to use for the jacket)
- Pattern paper, or other lightweight paper for drawing sewing pattern
- Ruler
- Pinking shears OR heavy-duty fabric scissors OR rotary cutter and cutting board
- Fabric pencil or tailor's chalk
- Tapestry needle and strong thread for assembly
- Yarn needle

Gauge

18 sts = 4 inches using MC on US #9/5.5mm needles in stockinette st (row gauge is not important for body pieces)

19 sts / 25 rows = 4 inches using CC on US #8/5mm needles in stockinette st

Patterns

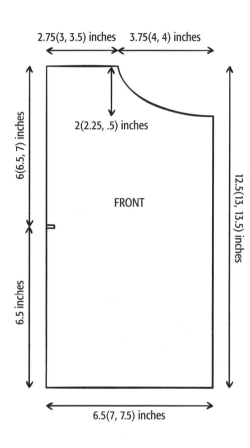

2.75(3, 3.5) inches   3.75(4, 4) inches

2(2.25, .5) inches

6(6.5, 7) inches

FRONT

12.5(13, 13.5) inches

6.5 inches

6.5(7, 7.5) inches

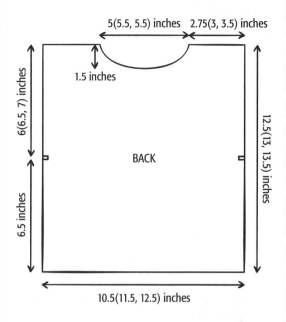

5(5.5, 5.5) inches   2.75(3, 3.5) inches

1.5 inches

6(6.5, 7) inches

BACK

12.5(13, 13.5) inches

6.5 inches

10.5(11.5, 12.5) inches

Instructions

Body Pieces (Make 2)

Using MC and US #9/5.5mm needles, CO 108 sts.

Work in stockinette st until you have used 2 full skeins of yarn.

BO all sts.

Sleeves (Make 2)

Using CC and US #8/5mm needles, CO 63[68, 73] sts.

Beginning with a WS row, work 3 rows in stockinette st.

Next Row [RS]: K1, k2tog, k to last 3 sts, ssk, k1.

Repeat these 4 rows 11 times more. 39[44, 49] sts remain.

Continue in stockinette st until work measures 8 inches, or 1 inch less than desired sleeve length. BO all sts.

Weave in ends.

Fulling

Full in the washing machine as directed in chapter 4, until fabric is very dense and individual stitches are no longer discernable. Two full cycles in the washing machine were necessary to achieve this density for the sample garment.

Lay pieces flat and allow to dry completely. This may take more than one day.

Determine which side of the fabric you prefer to use as the right side of the fabric, and mark accordingly.

Pattern Preparation

Use the measurements given in the pattern diagrams to draw paper pattern pieces for Back and one Front of jacket. Cut out pieces. Place Front piece onto another piece of paper, right side down. Trace and cut out this second Front piece; you should have two pieces which are mirror images of each other.

Fabric Preparation

Pin pattern pieces to fulled fabric and cut out. Use fabric pencil or tailor's chalk to transfer armhole markings to fabric.

Note: When cutting ribbing as directed below, be sure that it is oriented correctly! The depth should be measured along the ribs which compose the fabric, and the length should be measured perpendicular to the ribs.

Cuffs: Cut two pieces of ribbing which are 3 inches deep and 6[7, 8] inches long.

Waistband: Cut a piece of ribbing which is 4 inches deep and 19[21, 23] inches long.

Neckband: Cut a piece of ribbing which is 3 inches deep and 14.5[15.5, 16.75] inches long.

Assembly

Note: When sewing shoulder, sleeve, and side seams, leave a 0.25 inch seam allowance.

Pin fronts to back at shoulders, with right sides together. Sew shoulder seams.

Pin wide ends of sleeves to body, matching center of each sleeve to ends of shoulder seams, end edges of each sleeve to armhole marks. Sew in place.

Sew side seams and sleeve seams. Turn jacket right side out.

Note: When sewing ribbing, leave a 0.5 inch seam allowance.

Fold one piece of cuff ribbing in half, so that short edges are together. Sew short edges together. Fold one half of the resulting tube outwards and down over the other half of the tube, so that the long edges are together and the seam allowances are encased.

Slip cuff around end of one sleeve and pin cut edges of cuff to end of sleeve, stretching cuff to fit. Sew in place.

Repeat for other cuff.

Fold waistband in half so that long edges are together. Sew along each short edge. Turn waistband right side out; raw edges at ends of waistband are encased.

Pin cut edges of waistband along lower edge of jacket, stretching waistband to fit. Sew in place.

Fold neckband in half so that long edges are together. Pin long cut edges of neckband along neckline of jacket, stretching to fit, and curving ends of neckband towards edge of jacket, so that ribbing comes to a point at each side of center front (see photo). Sew in place and trim excess.

Finishing Instructions

Snaps

Use fabric pencil or tailor's chalk to mark placement of snaps on front edges of jacket. Be sure marks match exactly on right and left fronts!

Practice applying snaps by attaching 1 or 2 snaps to felt scraps from body pieces, following manufacturer's instructions.

Apply snaps to jacket.

Trim any uneven edges of felt pieces, and you're done!

Variation

The Rescued Sweater-Letter Jacket

You can save time and money on this project by using recycled knits as the fabric for your fronts and backs. Buy thrift-store sweaters (men's L or XL work well) ensuring that you have enough fabric. Be sure that the sweaters are 100 percent wool, and are not machine-washable. Full them in the machine, knit up the sleeves, and you're ready to put everything together. You can even buy an appliqué letter or use needle felting to embellish the front! You could also knit your own ribbing for the cuffs, waistband and neck instead of using commercial ribbing.

Loopy Boa

With bulky yarn and an 8mm crochet hook, you can start and finish this funky scarf in under an hour. Better yet, it's even suitable for first-time crocheters! All you need are three basic stitches; chain, slip stitch, and single crochet. You'll be set in a flash.

Project Rating: Flirtation

Cost: $15

Necessary Skills: ch (page 186); sc (page 187); sl st (page 187); sewing ends (page 194); fulling in the machine (page 50)

Abbreviations: ch-sp: the space made in the previous row by chaining one or more times between stitches

Finished Size:

Length: 56 inches
Width: Approx. 4 inches

Materials:

- MC: Brown Sheep Lamb's Pride Bulky (113g, 125 yd/ 114m, 85 percent wool, 15 percent mohair), Lotus Pink–1 skein
- CC: Brown Sheep Lamb's Pride Bulky (113g, 125 yd/ 114m, 85 percent wool, 15 percent mohair), Chianti–1 skein
- Substitution: Approximately 100m each in two colors of bulky feltable wool
- US L / 8mm crochet hook
- Yarn needle

Gauge

Gauge couldn't be less important for this project. Just make sure you can see air between your stitches for ease in fulling.

Instructions

MC Section

Using MC, ch 48. Working into the back loops of the chain, (skip first 5 ch, sl st in next ch) to end. 1 set of 8 loops has been made.

Without breaking yarn, *ch 54; working into the back loops of the chain, (skip first 5 ch, sl st in next ch) 8 times.* Second set of loops has been made, 6 ch left unworked.

Repeat from * to * 14 times more; 16 sets of loops have been made. Break yarn, draw through st on hook and pull tight.

You'll now switch to CC, and work staggered sets of loops. Don't worry about keeping the MC section untwisted as you work the CC section. By letting the CC motifs spiral around the MC section, you'll end up with a more interesting finished product!

CC Section

Use sl st to attach CC to base of set of loops at end of MC section. Ch 54. Working into the back loops of the chain, (skip first 5 ch, sl st in next ch) 8 times, sc in ch-6 space of MC section adjacent to last set of loops.

Without breaking yarn, *ch 54; working into the back loops of the chain, (skip first 5 ch, sl st in next ch) 8 times, sc in next ch6-sp of MC section.*

Repeat from * to * 13 times more; 15 sets of loops have been made. Ch 6. Sc in base of final set of loops of MC section. Break yarn, draw through st on hook and pull tight.

Finishing Instructions

Using yarn needle, loosely weave in ends to prevent unraveling.

Full in the washing machine as directed in chapter 4.

Hang or lay flat to dry.

Variation

Looking for a fuller boa? Why not work a few more sections like the CC Section? This pattern is also great for experimentation with yarn substitution. Use any thickness of yarn and just keep crocheting to make the scarf longer.

The pink and grey boa shown incorporates all of these variations: it is worked in a thinner alpaca yarn, for a very different texture from the wool boa, and it has two (pink) CC sections instead of one. If you substitute a different weight of yarn, be sure to match your hook size to the yarn. For example, while a bulky yarn needs an 8mm hook, a worsted weight yarn may fare better with a 6mm hook.

Sideways Striped Scarf

I love scarves, both as a fashion accessory and as a practicality here in Canada. As a knitter and crocheter, I'm used to waiting weeks to be able to wear a new home-made scarf. But, with wet felting, you can be ready to go the very next morning. Just make sure to hang it up to dry overnight. This design lets you play with color without the fuss; simply align the dyed fibers before felting. Even better, funky rope fringe adds a delightful touch. Need a scarf but not crazy about stripes? Use these project notes but stick with a single color of fiber, and you'll be ready to go tomorrow.

Project Rating: Summer Fling

Cost: Less than $20

Necessary Skills: Basic wet felting (page 17); felted ropes with frayed ends (page 24)

Finished Size

Length: 52 inches, excluding fringe
Width: 5 inches

Materials

- MC: merino fiber, approx 4 oz / 113g Ashland Bay Dyed Merino in sage
- CC: merino fiber, approx 3 oz / 85g Ashland Bay Dyed Merino in cranberry
- Wet felting supplies (see page 18)
- Sheet of bubble wrap, at least 60 inches by 24 inches (optional)

Instructions

Start by preparing the felted rope fringe. Following the instructions for felted rope on page 17, create six 10-inch fringes with MC and four with CC. Make sure to leave approximately 2 inches at the end of each rope completely dry and unfelted.

Prepare your working surface. For a scarf or other large piece of felt, I like working on a long sheet of bubble wrap, positioned with the bubbles down. This will add a bit of friction and speed up the felting process without overly abusing the wool.

Build three *very thin* layers of wool, switching between CC and MC to make the stripes as pictured. Aim for 58 inches long and 6 inches wide.

After placing the second layer, position fringe with 5 strands on each end of the scarf. As pictured, I made the colors line up so the MC fringe is positioned below the MC stripes and the CC fringe is next to the CC stripes.

Wet and felt as described in chapter 2.

inish by rolling vigorously in the bubble wrap or bamboo screen. (Consider also the *throw* approach. Hold the wet felt over your head and slam onto the floor or into a sink. This will further shock the wool.)

Finishing Instructions

inse to remove soap. Squeeze out any excess water. Hang overnight to dry.

Variation

Scarves are in many ways the perfect blank canvas. They use very little fiber, take less than an hour, start-to-finish, and provide you with a great new wearable the very next morning. Instead of sticking to stripes, consider using the three layers as a sandwich for a different type of fiber. This variation leaves out the fringe and uses natural white alpaca fiber and a thin layer of synthetic sparkly Firestar. The red Firestar shows through the sheer layer of alpaca and gives it a bit of interest.

Into felting beads? Try adding a few beads onto the surface before placing the top layer. You'll have a 3D texture that still reveals the colors of the wool beads.

Wild Thing Scarf

by Mandy Moore

This uniquely textured scarf juxtaposes two very different materials: earthy felted wool and ethereal organza. Wool yarn is sewn in a grid pattern onto the organza. The piece is then felted, which shrinks the yarn grid, ruching the fabric into sculptural bubbles or pockets. A short, tufted, felted fringe adds a final touch to this wild scarf.

Project Rating: Flirtation

Cost: Less than $30, depending on fabric cost

Necessary Skills: Fulling in the machine (page 50); basic hand sewing

Finished Size

Materials

- 0.75 yd / 0.65m synthetic organza, 60 inches / 150cm wide; shown in brown
- Cascade 220 (100g, 220 yd / 201m, 100 percent Peruvian highland wool), black–1 skein
- Substitution: Approx. 60 yd / 55m of worsted weight, feltable wool yarn.
- Sharp yarn needle
- Tape measure
- Scotch tape or masking tape or washable marker or straight pins to mark stitching lines on fabric

Pattern Notes

All sewing for this pattern is done using a simple running stitch. To work a running stitch, weave the needle in and out of the fabric in a straight line, making stitches which are more or less identical on each side of the fabric. For this project, stitches should be approx. 0.125 to 0.25 inches long. It is not important for the stitches to be of uniform length.

Instructions

Cut organza in half, cutting from selvage edge to selvage edge. You will have two pieces of fabric, each approx. 60 inches by 13.5 inches.

Cut a piece of yarn approx. 14 inches long, and thread it on the yarn needle. Overlap the selvage edge of the two pieces of fabric approx. 0.5 inch, and use the yarn to sew them together with a running stitch.

Using tape, marker, or pins, measure and mark a line 2 inches from, and parallel to, this first line of stitching. Cut a piece of yarn approx. 14 inches long, and sew along the marked line.

Continue in this manner, measuring, marking and sewing lines every 2 inches, until the entire length of the scarf has been worked. Run a line of stitching through the selvage edge at each end of the scarf.

easure and mark a line lengthwise, down the center of the scarf. It is helpful to measure the center point of each crosswise line of stitching. Sew along this line.

easure, mark and sew lines 2 inches out on either side of this center line, then lines 2 inches out from each of these lines. Five lengthwise lines of stitching have been worked.

ou will now have a very large organza scarf, slightly less than 10 feet long and approx. 13 inches wide, traversed by a grid of woolen stitching lines. Trim the yarn ends at the ends of each line of stitching, close to the edges of the fabric.

lace the scarf in a washing machine with a small amount of detergent and a pair of old jeans, or some other heavy garment. Do not use towels, or anything else that is likely to produce lint; it will get trapped in the ruffled folds of the felted scarf.

et the machine to hot wash / cold rinse, and run it through at least one cycle. The scarf will have shrunken considerably, and will have twisty, ruffly edges.

rim the outer 2 inches or so off each long edge of the scarf, cutting approx. ½ inch from the outermost lengthwise line of stitching on each side. This removes the ruffly unfinished edges from the long sides of the scarf and allows the ruffles to really show on the bottom (short) edges of the scarf.

Add Fringe

ut a piece of yarn approx. 5–6 inches long. Thread it on the needle and draw it through the end of a crosswise line of stitching, near the point where it intersects with the outermost lengthwise line of stitching. Tie it in a square knot, so that the ends are left hanging. Repeat this for each end of each crosswise line of stitching.

un the scarf through another cycle in the washing machine, to felt these short fringes. Trim any loose threads. Hang to dry.

Variation

Why not try this technique using different fabric? Chiffon, tulle, satin, lace, or a light cotton print will offer a different body and drape than organza. Have fun experimenting!

Scarf for the Subzero Urban Dweller

by Suzen Green

Felting onto a length of fabric lets you create a sturdy and warm neck wrap for the coldest winter days. Although you can choose any mesh-like fabric, I used a rust-dyed length of cream silk.

Project Rating: Summer Fling
Cost: $20–$50, depending on cost of fabric
Necessary Skills: Wet felting (page 17)

Finished Size

Length: Approx. 56 inches
Width: Approx. 12 inches

Materials

- 60 inches long by 13 inches wide of silk chiffon (pre-washed)
- 50g of carded wool roving (merino or Corriedale)
- 1 large bamboo window blind with metal attachments removed
- 5 yd or two 2.5 yd pieces of bubble wrap
- Murphy's Oil Soap
- Large towels
- Small bucket to hold hot soapy water
- Rubber gloves suitable for working with hot water
- Large sponge
- Plastic drop cloth or table cloth

Instructions

Cover your work area with a plastic drop cloth and place at least one large towel on your working surface; the towel will soak up any excess water from the felting process and make cleaning up quick.

Place the bamboo blind on top of the towels and spread out the bubble wrap, bubble-side up on top of the bamboo blind. Place the 1.5 yds of silk chiffon lengthwise on top of the bubble wrap.

Using a small amount of roving, begin placing a thin layer of fleece on top of the silk chiffon as directed in chapter 2. A small amount of fleece extending over the edge of the silk ends up looking naturally frayed rather than sharply cut.

Apply a second thin layer of fleece on top of the first, making sure the fibers are positioned at a 90 degree angle to the first layer. The fibers of this layer should create a cross or T-shape with the layer of fiber below it.

Combine a capful of Murphy's Oil Soap with very hot water in a small bucket. The water should be sudsy and a little cloudy. With a gloved hand, dip your sponge into the bucket but do not ring out. Place the soapy sponge firmly onto the prepared scarf,

condensing the fleece. Be careful not to lift or shift the fleece fibers. Continue to wet the fleece with the sponge until the entire scarf surface is flat and saturated. You may have to refill your water bucket if you run short. Just be careful to avoid over-wetting the scarf. The surface should be entirely wet, but not drowning.

When the scarf surface is wet, fold the bubble wrap over the scarf, sandwiching it between the bubbles. Working from one end, roll the bamboo blind up like a cinnamon roll, rolling the bubble-wrapped scarf up with it. Continue to roll the bamboo back and forth like a rolling pin. The textured surfaces of the bamboo and bubble wrap will agitate and felt the fleece fibers through the silk chiffon. Unroll the bamboo and check the scarf: if one end seems to be felting more quickly than the other, roll the bamboo from the opposite side to even it out.

After a few minutes of rolling, check to see whether the wool fibers have attached to the silk. To do this, gently try to separate the wool from the silk. If the fibers are sticking together, then you can remove the bubble wrap and continue rolling the scarf in the bamboo mat. It is important to make sure that the fibers are attaching together before removing the bubble wrap; otherwise the fibers may wrap around the bamboo and tangle while you are rolling.

When the fleece has successfully felted to the silk, remove the scarf from the bamboo screen and hold it by the middle. Drop the scarf continuously on the textured surface of the opened bamboo blind to simulate the tumble cycle of a clothes dryer. Repeat this for five or ten minutes. It's a great way to release all the day's frustrations!

Note: Be mindful of checking the scarf as you do this "pick-up and drop" action because it will cause the scarf to shrink quite rapidly. You don't want your scarf to shrink up too much or become too stiff.

Finishing Instructions

When you are satisfied with how the scarf has felted, it is time to wash out the excess soap. Do this by hand-washing with a mild soap just as you would any hand-knit wool garment.

Hang to dry.

Variation

Play around with color by felting with contrasting fleece and silk. For example if you use a blue silk chiffon and a yellow fleece, you'll end up with a greenish hue to your scarf on the silk side. Have fun with patterns by using a printed silk mesh or even use cheesecloth if silk chiffon is unavailable to you. Apply just one layer of fleece and enjoy a scarf with a lot more drape or add more fleece for a very stiff stole.

Featherweight Scarf

Thick felt is easy to make, but creating a lightweight, almost-sheer fabric can be a bit trickier. Experiment with this funky design, felted down from a thin lattice-design. As shown, we used a drapey and soft, pure, alpaca fiber and overdyed the finished product.

Project Rating: **Summer Fling**

Cost: **Less than $20**

Necessary Skills: **Basic wet felting (page 17); felted ropes with frayed ends (page 24); dyeing (page 75)**

Finished Size

Length: 46 inches
Width: 12 inches

Materials

- MC: alpaca fiber, approx 4 oz /113g, un-dyed
- Wet felting supplies (see page 18)
- Sheet of bubble wrap, at least 60 inches by 24 inches (optional)
- Acid dye and dye supplies (see page 68)

Instructions

Prepare your lattice design following the lines in the following figure. As shown, begin with the 4 long horizontal lines of fiber. These should be approximately 48 inches long, 1 inch wide, and spaced 3 inches apart. Lay the fiber in the direction of the line, not perpendicular to it.

Next, build the 16 vertical lines to connect into a grid. These should also be positioned evenly along the width of the scarf, and approximately 1 inch thick.

Repeat a second layer of the horizontal lines, then a second layer of the vertical lines.

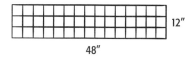

Wet and felt as described in chapter 2.

Note: Just after applying the soapy water, you'll want to use your fingers to push the stray fibers back into the grid shape. You'll have the best results if the fibers are fairly *stacked* into the right shape.

Finish by rolling vigorously in the bubble wrap or bamboo screen.

Consider also the throw approach. Hold the wet felt over your head and slam onto the floor or into a sink. This will further shock the wool.

Finishing Instructions

Rinse to remove soap. Squeeze out any excess water.

n your dye pot, add enough water to cover the scarf, then stock dye solution, then salt. We used 6 L of water and 300ml of stock solution and a quarter cup of salt. Stir well. Then, add wet scarf. With the heat on medium-low, bring to a gentle boil and let simmer for 30 minutes.

emove the scarf from the pot and set aside. Add 500ml of white vinegar and stir well. Replace the scarf into the pot and continue to simmer for an additional 30 minutes.

urn off the burner and let the pot sit until the water is room temperature.

emove the scarf, empty the dye pot, and wash everything well in gentle soap. Hang or lay flat to dry.

Variation

Instead of a lightweight drapey scarf, consider using a more dense fiber, such as wool. In the photographed variation, we used two different colors of dyed merino from Ashland Bay fibers; one color for each of the two grid layers. We also made only 3 horizontal bands of fiber in the grid portion; therefore it is quite a bit skinnier.

Swing Raglan

When I first felted a swatch of this silk/alpaca blend, I instantly thought of how cozy this would feel as a garment. Both warm and lightweight, it seemed ideally suited for a loose cardigan/jacket with cropped sleeves. It seemed perfect over a turtleneck for winter, or as a lightweight layer for cool summer nights. Even better, as an easy sewing project, this cardigan is simple to adapt to your measurements.

Project Rating: Love o' Your Life

Cost: Less than $40 for fiber

Necessary Skills: Wet felting (page 17); machine sewing

Finished Size

Fits a 36–40 inch chest measurement. The fit is meant to be loose and swingy! For a larger size, use the same proportions but cut the body pieces wider.

Materials

- Approx. 1 lb of fiber. We used a 30/70 tussah/alpaca blend from Ashland Bay.
- 2 large sheets of paper, at least 24 by 20 inches
- Yard stick
- Straight pins
- Scissors or rotary cutter
- Iron with steam setting
- Sewing machine, with matching thread and heavy-duty needle

Instructions

Following wet felting directions in chapter 2, pages 28 through 32, make two 24 by 24 inch squares of 5 layers of fiber. Next, make a third sheet of fabric, approx. 24 by 40 inches If the larger sheets are too difficult or frustrating, you could alternatively felt two 24 by 20 inch rectangles. If possible, err on the side of creating larger sheets. Some shrinkage will occur during felting, and it's essential to be able to cut out the pattern pieces. Remember, if making a larger size, you'll need larger sheets of felt.

Note: It's not important to have straight or even edges, as any excess will be trimmed.

Hang and let dry. When fully dry, press with a steam iron to smooth the surface.

Now, you'll want to decide whether you need to make any pattern alterations. If you want to make a wider jacket, you'll draw the following pattern pieces larger in width than indicated. For example, to sew a jacket with a 44-inch finished chest measurement, the back piece will need to be 23 inches wide to allow for seam allowances. It may be helpful to use a sheet of broadcloth or muslin to test out your pattern pieces on store-bought fabric before using your carefully crafted felt.

ake a raglan template for the back as follows. Draw a rectangle of 22 inches wide by 10 inches tall. Divide in half at center to make two 11 by 10 inch rectangles. Draw center line 10 inches higher. Working at a 90-degree angle to the center line, draw a line that extends 4 inches on either side of the center line. Connect the edge of the rectangle with the end of the 8-inch line on both sides. Your template should look like the following figure. This is the template for the back and front of your jacket.

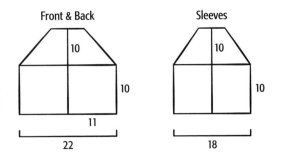

Front & Back   Sleeves

ow, create the template for the sleeves. First, draw a rectangle of 18 inches wide by 10 inches tall. Divide in half at the center as before. Extend the center line 10 inches higher. As before, draw a line that extends 2 inches on either side of the center line.

eginning with the back, pin the template onto a sheet of 24 by 24 inch felt and use scissors or a rotary cutter to cut

out. Next, pin the same template onto a second 24 by 24 inch sheet of felt and cut out again. Cut up the center to create two fronts. Similarly, use the sleeve template to cut out two sleeves from the larger square of felt.

Finishing Instructions

hoose which side of each piece you'd like facing inward. This will be called the "wrong side" from now on. The side that will face the world will be called the "right side."

ow, with the right sides together, sew the sleeves to the back at the diagonal raglan seams, using a ⅜ inch seam allowance. Since the jacket is unhemmed, you'll want to reinforce all seams at both ends. Next, sew the fronts to the sleeves at the raglan seams. At this point, it should more or less look like a jacket! Fold so the side seams are together and the underarm edges line up. Sew the side seams and underarms on both sides. Press the seams open with the steam iron.

urn right side out. Matching your previous seams, sew another line of stitching ¼ inch apart from all seams, attaching the seam allowance to the body of the jacket.

Variation

Do you sew? You can make flat wool felt fabric to use with many commercial sewing patterns. How do you know whether the pattern is a good fit for the fabric? Look for sewing patterns that recommend heavy-duty fabrics like canvas. Some coat or jacket patterns do suggest boiled wool, which is essentially wool felt.

Alternatively, draft your own simple patterns, as we did in this project. Want more tapered sleeves? Draw the sleeve template with a gentle slope from underarm to cuff. Want buttons on the front? Cut and reinforce buttonholes down one side and sew buttons to the other. Want a wrap jacket instead? When cutting out the front pieces, instead draw a diagonal line from the shoulder to a point halfway between the arm shaping and the bottom hem. Just remember, if you're making alterations like this, you'll need more felt.

Chapter Eight

◆◆◆

Quick Gifts & Oddities

The Save-Your-Marriage Knitting Needle Roundup

Keep those needles in check with this recycled sweater project.

Spring Is Sprung!

Needle felt some happy blooms for your lapel.

Chunky Bead Necklace

Beaders love felt too! Felted beads make great additions to chunky necklaces.

Fishin' for Kittens

Your cat will love this needle-felted fish toy.

Uber Chunky Felted Yarn

Make your own super chunky felted yarn by fulling a skein of finger-crocheted yarn.

Moleskine Jacket

Cover your Moleskine notebook in style.

In Stitches Earrings

Slow cookers aren't just for making dinner anymore! Use yours to create a cute pair of earrings.

The Save-Your-Marriage Knitting Needle Roundup

by Cindy Kitchel

Several months ago, someone in our house shrunk a few of my tried-and-true wool sweaters by throwing them in the washer (on hot, no less) and dryer. There will be no finger pointing, but I'm fairly certain the guilty party was not me but wears a wedding ring that matches mine. Since no amount of dieting would render the sweaters wearable, I recycled my old friends into this handy knitting holder. After I figured out the best way to sleekly attach the felted sweater pieces to holder, this project was a breeze to make, requiring only remedial measuring and sewing skills. Tragedy averted; marriage saved.

Project Rating: Summer Fling

Cost: About $15 for fabric and supplies, assuming the felted sweaters are free and from your closet; if you have to pick some up at a thrift store, about $25.

Necessary Skills: Using a sewing machine; hand sewing; fulling in the machine (page 50)

Finished Size

Height: 9 inches
Width: 26 inches when opened up; about 7 inches when folded

Materials

- Two or more fairly thin, 100 percent wool sweaters; your basic Lands End sweater in a plain stitch (no fancy, bulky cables) is a good place to start
- 1½ yd sturdy fabric, like denim or upholstery fabric
- Thread
- Hand-sewing needle
- Tailor's chalk
- Double-stick fusible web, such as Steam-A-Seam 2
- Liquid stitch glue, such as Unique Stitch
- 1 yard coordinating ribbon
- If wanted, buttons or other decorations
- Sewing machine
- Iron and ironing board

Instructions

Cut the material into four pieces:

- Front: 10 inches high by 27 inches long
- Back: 10 inches high by 27 inches long
- Pocket holder: 14 inches high by 27 inches long
- Top flap: 10 inches high by 27 inches long

Fold the pocket holder in half, wrong sides together. Align the pocket holder on the bottom of the front piece, right sides together. Pin these pieces together.

Using tailor's chalk, mark your sewing lines. Here's the basic scheme (take a look at the diagram if this isn't making sense). In the very middle of the holder, mark two rows of stitching about ½ inch apart. This is your main fold line.

Mark the rest of the pockets and fold lines:

- To the right of the main fold line, mark three more lines, each 2 inches apart from each other. From this last line, mark a line ¼ inch apart. Now mark two more lines 2 inches apart from each other. You now have marked, to the right, six 2 inch pockets and a secondary fold line.

- To the left of the main fold line, mark four more lines, each 1½ inches apart from each other. From this last line, mark a line ¼ inch apart. Now mark three more lines 1½ inches apart from each other. You now have marked, to the right, eight 1½ inch pockets and a secondary fold line.

Stitch on your drawn lines.

Lay the front over the back, right sides together, and sew them together like a pillow, using a ½ inch seam and leaving about a 6 inch opening at the top so that you can turn it right side out. When you finish sewing, turn the holder right side out and press it well, making the corners as crisp as you can and turning under the opening at the top of the holder.

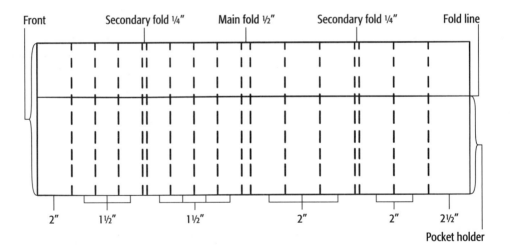

Fold the top flap in half longwise, right sides together, and sew a ½ inch seam around the three open sides, leaving about a 6 inch opening at the top so that you can turn it right side out. When you finish sewing, turn the flap right side out and press it well, making the corners as crisp as you can and turning under the opening at the top of the flap.

Sew around side and bottom edges of the flap, as shown, sewing in ¼ inch from the edge. See the following diagram.

Lay the flap over the holder; the open edges of both should be at the top. Sew a line ¼ inch from the edge, securing the two pieces together and closing the open edges. Now your holder's done and you're ready to move on to felting it!

Cut the double-stick fusible web to a size that completely covers the back of your holder; this is what you'll use to cement the felted sweaters to your holder. You'll likely need to cut several pieces of the web to cover the holder. Now lay the sweater pieces as you want them on the holder. You might want to go with symmetrical rectangles, stripes, a crazy-quilt variety with pieces fitting together as they're able, or some other fun design. Just be sure that you cut the pieces so that the edges fit exactly together; don't overlap the sweater pieces.

When you have the pieces as you want them, follow the manufacturer's instructions for ironing the pieces together. Generally, you'll be holding the iron in place about 15 to 20 seconds, picking it up, and then holding the iron on the next spot until you've secured all of the pieces. Wool is tough to get completely secure using only the double-stick fusible web, so you'll next be securing all ends with liquid stitch glue.

Run a thin line of liquid stitch glue under all of the sweater edges, smearing it with your finger and holding down the edges to secure them. Follow the manufacturer's instructions after you've secured the ends; you'll often need to let the piece dry for about 24 hours.

When the piece is dry, fold the two ends of the holder toward the middle, on the secondary fold lines. Now fold the whole thing in two on the main fold line.

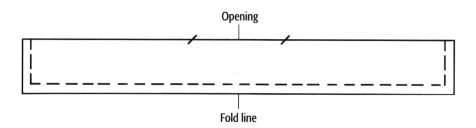

Opening

Fold line

Cut the ribbon in half and, using a hand needle, secure it to the sides of the folded needle case so that you can tie up the case when you're not using it. Be sure that when you sew on the ribbon, you sew through one layer of the holder fabric and not just through the felted sweater layer; this will keep you from tearing the felted sweater cover and will keep the ribbon secure.

Use your decorations to customize your needle case further. For mine, I sewed old buttons (two grey ones actually came from one of the felted sweaters!) onto free-form flowers cut from another felted sweater that was too thick to use in this project. Then I used the liquid stitch glue to glue the flowers onto the front of my holder.

Load up with needles, and get knitting!

Variation

Another clever way to hold crafting tools is with a needle roll, and the pattern for a roll is almost the same as the folded holder. The roll is more appropriate for crochet hooks or single-point needles, in which you'll only have two needles per pocket. To make a roll, follow the same instructions, but make these adjustments:

- Don't stitch the fold lines; instead, make all stitching lines between pockets single lines.
- To sew on the ribbon, simply fold it in half, and at that fold mark, secure it to one end of the holder. You'll roll up the holder from the other end, and then tie the two ends of the ribbon around the roll.
- To make a single-pointed knitting needle holder, you'll need exactly 2 yd of fabric. Because I'm a pessimist who always likes a little give, I'd purchase 2½ yd, but that's just me. Cut the front, back, and flap 17 inches high and 29 inches wide. Cut the pocket 21 inches high and 29 inches wide. You can draw and sew the pocket lines any way you like. If, for example, you like symmetry, can you draw and sew eight 1½ inch pockets and eight 2 inch pockets.
- To make a crochet hook holder, you'll need ½ yd of fabric. Cut the front, back, and flap 8 inches high and 15 inches wide. Cut the pocket 11 inches high and 15 inches wide. Draw and sew the pocket lines any way you like to accommodate your hook collection.

Spring Is Sprung!

by Karen Harper

Whether you live in the arctic and get used to months and months of winter, or you spend the harsher months on a sunny beach, everyone can use a little bloom. These needle-felted blossoms fit the bill, adding much-needed color without wilting from the cold. What more can you ask from a flower?

Project Rating: Flirtation

Cost: Less than $10

Necessary Skills: Hand sewing; needle felting (page 47)

Finished Size

Large posy with leaves: approx. 3 by 3 inches

Small posy: 2 by 2 inches

Materials

- Small amounts of dyed fiber in several colors . . . less than 1 oz each color
- 1 stick or bar pin for the back of each flower
- At least one felting needle. We used 38-gauge star-shaped needles for this project.
- 12 by 12 inch piece of foam, at least 2 inches thick.
- Sewing thread and needle to attach pin back. Alternatively, heavy-duty fabric glue.

Instructions

Note: When needle felting 3-D objects, most of the success is in the inspiration. If you can imagine a shape, you can needle felt it. Remember, as we discussed in chapter 3, nothing is set in stone. Want a larger flower? Use more fiber, or add more layers as you go! Following are instructions for re-creating the blooms we photographed. It will be helpful to reference the photos as you work, if you want to make similar flowers.

Large Posy

Taking the main color you want your posy to be, make a puff of it in your hand, about 20 percent bigger than you want the finished product to be. Form it into a little patty-shaped piece and place on foam.

Get set for the poking and stabbing. This is a good way to release some of your daily frustrations! You will want to start on the outside and stab around the perimeter, keeping the edges as neat as you can. Do a full pass over the whole thing until it's a little flattened circle on your foam. Now pick it up and flip it over. Do it again. You can keep doing this until it starts to take shape, paying attention to the edges as you go. You will see the flower/circle starting to take shape pretty soon, and it will harden up, reduce in size, and start to feel like felt. When you feel slight resistance, you know you are on your way.

ow you can start to shape the petals. You take your needle and push into the edge where you want the delineation for each petal to be. Keep poking until you have achieved the depth of petal you want. You can also go down each length of petal to give more definition. Put this aside for now.

Leaves

sing the same technique, lay out the fiber for the leaves. Needle felt first around the outside, watching your edges. Then, move into the center until the fiber has shrunken and is holding a leaf shape.

se the felting needle to attach the leaves to the flower. Slip the leaves under the posy, positioning them where you want them. Then—holding the leaves in place—flip the posy over so that it and the leaves are face down. Needle felt the leaves to the posy, making sure you connect all areas. Flip over and continue needle felting from the front.

t this point, the leaves and flowers should be very hard to pull apart, and there should be no green from the back showing. If there is, you can cover it with a small amount of your main color. Now you can add definition to the leaves if you want. Small veins look really cute!

ow that you have completed your blossom body, its time to embellish it as you want. You can add small amounts of contrasting or complimentary color along the petals. You can also take small amounts of fiber and roll them up into tiny balls to add to the center of your flower. If you're into sparkly, consider adding some sequins with sewing thread!

Small Posy

o make a smaller flower, work as for the large posy but with less fiber. When you are at the slight resistance stage, take your secondary color and add small bumps of color directly to the main color to simulate another set of petals. Keep adding until you are satisfied with the look and continue to define the petals of both colors until you like it. For an optional bit of texture, add three small contrasting balls to the center of piece and felt well.

Finishing Instructions

ew the pin to the back of the flower securely. Wear with reckless abandon!

Variation

3-D felting is only limited by what you can dream. Karen also whipped up a little pink skull pin, using the same techniques. Why not make tiny cupcakes? Or needle felt your initial for a Laverne and Shirley flashback. Since needle felting uses so little fiber and takes so little time, use it as a chance to play.

Chunky Bead Necklace

by Becky Wright, instructions transcribed by Roxane Cerda

This funky chunky beaded necklace is a great way to experiment with hand-felted beads. While we used a mix of different textures for this project, raid your own bead stash (or your local bead store) for your own individual mix of beads. Then, wet felt as many wooly beads as you'd like.

Project Rating: Flirtation

Cost: $15–$25, depending on your materials

Necessary Skills: Bead stringing (we'll walk you through this), wet felting beads (page 26)

Materials

- Wool roving in assorted colors. 1 oz makes one large bead or a few smaller ones.
- All-purpose felting needles
- 4 large, glass rondelles (disk-shaped beads with a hole through the center)
- 4 large, green wooden rondelles
- 8 large, brown wooden rondelles, slightly smaller than the green ones you selected above
- 2 large copper, metallic colored round beads, approximately 18mm
- 2 large, round, green, wooden beads, approximately 12mm
- 4 large flat, oval shaped wooden beads (approximately 28mm) with a top-to-bottom hole through the center
- 18 faux hematite rondelles, approximately 2mm wide, and 5mm across
- 12 orange round wooden beads, approximately 8mm

- tiger tail bead stringing wire (approximately 36")
- 2 sterling silver beads, approximately 2mm
- 2 sterling silver crimp beads
- 1 clasp of your choice
- Chain nose pliers
- Crimping pliers
- Wire cutters

Instructions

Wet felt the beads, shaping them into balls, as directed on pages 26–27 of chapter 2.

Using a bead reamer, felting needle, or just the tiger tail wire, pierce through each bead.

Pull the length of tiger tail wire from your spool, leaving it attached to the spool.

Arrange all of your beads in the order in which you would like them to be on the finished piece. To copy the finished piece here, follow the photo in the color insert.

tarting at one end, string all of your beads onto the tiger tail, beginning and ending with one of the small, 2mm sterling silver beads.

dd one of the crimp beads, and one side of your chosen clasp. Bring the end of the tiger tail back through the crimp bead, until you have a tail of approximately 1 inch. Using your crimping pliers, secure the clasp to the string by crushing the crimp bead first in the slot deepest in the pliers jaw, then again, this time in the slot closest to the tip of the jaw.

nip the excess wire down to about ¼ inch and slip the end into the first bead or two in the string.

ut the necklace off of the spool of wire, leaving about 6" to work with. Add the other crimp beads, and the other side of your clasp. Bring the end of the tiger tail back through the crimp bead, working it through until your clasp is worked closely to your necklace. You should still be able to coil your necklace, so don't pull the wire too tightly! Using your crimping pliers, secure

the clasp to the string by crushing the crimp bead the same way you did on the other end.

nip the excess wire, leaving a tail about ¼ inch long. To conceal the tail, work it into the first bead or two on your necklace.

n each hand, hold one end of your necklace, pull up to your neck, and then around, securing the clasp at the back. **Sway** to and fro in front of a mirror and envision all of the oohs and ahhs your new creation will bring.

Variation

Does your swanky new necklace leave your wrists weeping in jealousy? Follow the same instructions to make a stranded bracelet. Even better, the wooly felted beads won't make your wrists ache at the end of the day. They're lightweight, soft, and non-abrasive.

Fishin' for Kittens

by Karen Harper

Not having a cat, I had to rely on getting dog approval for this. Max says YES to things that flail about, and this fishy didn't disappoint. He likes a toy that smiles back. Really, who wouldn't? Please be careful with all toys, and if you notice fibers starting to pop up or off, make sure you take it away from kitty (or doggy) and ensure that loose fibers aren't a choking hazard. Trim or re-felt as needed.

Project Rating: Summer Fling

Cost: Under $10

Necessary Skills: Needle felting (page 47)

Finished Size

4½ inches long, 2½ inches across, 1½ inches thick (approx.)

Materials

- 2 oz or so of uncarded fiber, natural color
- Bits of colored roving, wool, or fiber to decorate your fishy
- Long piece of strong yarn or string to ensure fun flailing
- Darning needle big enough to use with your desired string or yarn
- Needle felting supplies (page 44)

Instructions

Take your uncarded fiber and form it into a palm-sized, slightly flattened oval. You can actually rub your hands together (like you are washing your hands) to start a little of the felting process and get your fiber to hold together.

Place the fiber on the needle felting foam and begin to poke it with the needle. You will want to start stabbing near the outside edge of the fiber, keeping the edges as neat as you can. Do a full pass over the whole thing with the needle until the fiber is slightly flattened.

Now pick it up and flip it over. Repeat the circular stabbing. You will see the fishy starting to take shape pretty soon, and it will start to harden up, reduce in size, and start to feel like felt. Continue until you feel a slight resistance.

Now, mark an indent about two thirds of the way across the fish for the start of the tail.

When your fishy has started to firm up nicely, you can add more fiber to round him out. Keep him nice and round, going over him with more fiber (wrapping it around his belly and head to keep it filled out), rolling him around your foam to get all sides and the front as needed. Leave the tail section alone until his body is as chubby as you want it. DO NOT OVER-FELT, AS IT WILL BE DIFFICULT TO ADD DECORATION TO REALLY HARD FELT. Keep the body slightly flexible for now.

Work the tail section as you did the body, but it should remain slightly flatter than the body. Put a small dent in the back edge so it looks like the top of a heart and felt more fiber to the sides to puff out the fins a bit. The tail should be about two thirds of the thickness of the body.

When you're happy with the final shape of your fish, go ahead and add colored fiber for embellishments. Use the picture for reference or let your imagination run wild. Zebra fish, clown fish . . . you decide. The most important part of this is up to you and your pet.

After you have applied all the colored fiber you want to use, you need to needle felt it until it is quite hard. NOW IS THE TIME TO OVER-FELT! You will want to ensure that all loose fibers are as tacked down and firm as they can be. I can't stress enough the importance of this step. Loose fibers can and will cause kitty or doggy to choke, so make sure this is a really hard felt.

Finishing Instructions

Thread a darning needle with string or yarn and poke it through where the tail meets body. Tie it firmly into a circle at the length you desire and then fling it about—to you and your pet's delight. If you want, instead of tying a circle, you can even attach the string or yarn fishing-line-style to a length of dowel for better "casting."

Variation

You could make a whole school of these and use them as a mobile. Try adding beads and sequins to embellish them, or even make an octopus or star fish to join them. If using beads, do not let fishy come into contact with your pet. Beads and pets don't mix. Trust me.

Uber Chunky Felted Yarn

Take a couple of balls of stash yarn and finger crochet a long cord. Then, skein it up and throw it in the wash. Et Voila! Super-Chunky Felted Yarn! With this project, don't be afraid to play. Combine a felting yarn and a synthetic and see what happens. Or take two worsted-weight yarns to felt into a standard chunky yarn. But beware! This one is highly addictive and quicker than you think. The skein shown took me less than 10 minutes to whip up!

Project Rating: Flirtation

Cost: $20 to make one skein of yarn, even less if you're stash-diving!

Necessary Skills: fulling in the machine (page 50)

Finished Size:

Yields approximately 30 yards/26m of yarn before felting.

After felting, skein will shrink slightly to approximately 22 yards/20m.

Materials

- MC: Brown Sheep Lamb's Pride Bulky (113g, 125 yd/114m, 85 percent wool, 15 percent mohair), Onyx–1 skein
- CC1: Brown Sheep Lamb's Pride Bulky (113g, 125 yd/114m, 85 percent wool, 15 percent mohair), Persian Turquoise–1 skein
- CC2: Madil Kid Seta (25g, 240 yrds/210m, 70 percent kid mohair, 30 percent silk), Color 462–1 ball
- Substitution: Approximately 115m each in three types or colors of yarn. Here's where creativity will come in handy!
- 10m of a nonfelting wool to use for tying your skein

Instructions

With three strands of yarn, make a slip knot. Finger-crochet the strands as follows:

Insert right thumb, index, and middle finger through the loop. With thumb and middle finger, grab three strands of yarn and pull through to make another loop. Repeat until all yarn is used, pulling final yarn all the way through final loop and pulling tight to make a knot. To make a longer skein, just tie knots from the old yarn to the new yarn and keep crocheting. The knots will felt right into the "yarn."

Finishing Instructions

Wind into a skein using a skein winder, two outstretched hands, or the back of a chair. Using superwash scrap yarn, tie the skein LOOSELY but SECURELY at several points. Make sure to secure the ends of the skein as well.

Full in the washing machine as directed in chapter 4. While the skein is still wet, with your hands, fluff out the individual chained strands so they do not stick together. Still in a skein, pull tightly on both ends of the skein to stretch. Hang to dry.

Variation

Is your mind racing with fab ideas for this technique? We used two strands of wool/mohair, and one thin strand of silk/mohair that added texture without bulk. What would happen if you chose two strands of wool and a strand of eyelash or ribbon yarn? How about creating your own self-striping yarn by switching colors every once in awhile?

But, what will you do with your newly created yarn? As you read in part 1 of this book, wool felt is extremely strong and water resistant. How about a bulky winter hat? Or a small handbag? The yarn you made will knit to around 1.5 stitches per inch. Look for patterns or design your own! It's up to you!

Moleskine Jacket

The ubiquitous black Moleskine notebook has become more than a practicality; it's a fashion statement. Although you can certainly adorn yours with stickers and stencils, why not wet felt a marble-effect book jacket?

Project Rating: Flirtation

Cost: $10, plus the notebook cost (even less if you dye the fleece yourself)

Necessary Skills: Needle felting on a flat surface (page 47); wet felting using a resist (page 34); felted rope with frayed ends (page 24)

Finished Size

Fits an 8 inch by 6 inch Moleskine note-book

Materials

- Approximately 50g of dyed fiber. Shown: Spunky Eclectic BFL in "Burning Embers."
- Handful of black or grey wool for the button cord. Shown: Lorna's Laces Wool Top in "Black Purl."
- Less than a meter of black or grey yarn for the details. Shown: Brown Sheep Lamb's Pride Worsted, "Onyx."
- Wet felting supplies (see page 18)
- Approx. 8 by 16 inch piece of plastic for resist
- Black 1.5 inch button for front closure
- 8 by 6 inch notebook. We used one from Moleskine. (Want a different size? Adjust the size of the template when you trace it below.)

Instructions

Cut the plastic to the correct dimensions for the book cover. The most effective way to do this is to open your notebook on top of the piece of plastic and trace an outline approximately 1 inch wider on all edges than the book itself. Mark the position of the spine on the template. You'll later use this to determine where to stop the folded in edge.

Form the button loop. From the contrasting color of fiber, pull an 8-inch length of fiber approximately the diameter of your thumb. Roll slightly to condense the fibers. Soak the center 4 inches of the cord in warm water. Lay the cord on your textured mat and roll the center until it becomes quite dense and felted. Make sure to keep the ends dry! When the center is fully felted, use your fingers to fray the dry ends.

Position the plastic resist template in the middle of your working surface. Layer the main color of fiber over the template, leaving 2 inches of overlap on the two side edges as well as on the top and bottom 4 inches from each side edge. These will later be folded in to create the flaps the notebook will slide into. Build 4 layers as suggested on page 28 ("Building Your Layers").

Add the soapy water to the middle portion of the mat, being careful to again leave the edges dry. Press the water into the fiber until fully saturated. Push in any stray fibers from the top and bottom edges of the book. Your goal should be to ensure that the fiber overlaying the template is wet and the 2 inches extra are still dry. Gently rub to begin felting the wet fibers together. When the piece feels secure enough, flip over so the felt is underneath the template.

old in the fiber on all edges. Insert the frayed edges of the cord into the middle of one of the folds to create the button hole. This will wrap around the book to secure to a toggle on the front cover. Add fiber in 4 layers to cover the template from both sides, leaving the center 3 inches of the template uncovered. Push in any stray fibers to leave a smooth edge. Pay special attention to the corners of the book. You'll want these to be amply covered with fiber to prevent holes from wearing through.

horoughly soak the fibers on this side of the book jacket as well. Felt as described on page 30 ("Adding Friction"). When fibers successfully pass the "pinch test" (see page 31), remove the template from the jacket and continue to hand-felt. Roll the felt up in bamboo mat and roll back and forth until the felt has shrunk. Rotate the jacket 90 degrees and repeat the rolling until you are satisfied with the final texture of the jacket.

inse carefully in room-temperature water to rinse any remaining soap. Don't wring the felt; it will stretch and distort the fabric. Instead, use your hands to roll and gently squeeze the felt to remove the excess water as much as possible. Or, use a dry towel to press out the water.

lock your book jacket to stretch it into the right size and shape for the notebook. While the jacket is still wet, place your notebook in a series of plastic bags and stretch the jacket to fit around the notebook. Leave on to dry.

Note: To speed up the drying process and help avoid water damage to your notebook, leave the jacket-covered notebook in the sun or in a breezy spot.

Finishing Instructions

have or steam block the felt to the desired texture. Sew button on front of jacket with a sewing needle and thread.

ith a felting needle and a strand of yarn, attach the black yarn to the front cover as shown.

Variation

The same technique can be applied to create unusual, one-of-a-kind covers for scrapbooks, photo albums, and even CD holders. Before beginning, just cut the plastic template to the correct shape, remembering to add an extra 1 in. or so on all sides to allow for shrinkage.

Alternatively, make your book jacket into a portable bag. In addition to the button rope, you can roll-felt a long enough cord to make a sturdy strap. For this, you'll want a cord at least 36 inches long and 1 inch in diameter after felting. Don't forget to leave the dry ends as directed previously! When layering the felt for the body of the book jacket, incorporate the dry ends of the strap into both sides of where the book spine will be positioned. Make sure to very securely felt these ends in place, and you'll have a fabulous and very functional book/bag.

In Stitches Earrings

by Roxane Cerda

Felt makes an ideal surface for stitched-on decorations. Check out this embellished earring project. Although you can make the felt as you learned in part 1 of this book, for this project we used your everyday slow cooker to speed things along. Got the itch to stitch? Check out *Not Your Mama's Stitching* (Wiley Publishing, Inc., 2007) for more great projects!

Project Rating: Flirtation

Cost: $20

Necessary Skills: Embroidery; needle felting (page 47)

Materials

- 100 percent wool roving (We chose a variegated brown for ours.)
- Slow cooker or large bowl
- Dish soap
- Kitchen towel
- Kitchen tongs
- Shears
- Embroidery scissors
- 1 skein brown (DMC #3031) embroidery floss (or color to match roving)
- 1 skein ivory (DMC Ecru) embroidery floss
- Embroidery needle, size 5
- Felting needle
- Chain nose pliers
- Foam block (You'll use this to support your piece during the part of the felting process that involves stabbing the felt over and over and over, like Norman Bates.)
- 2 ear wires
- 2 closed jump rings, 5 mm

Pattern Note

This pattern uses a slow cooker to wet felt the earring bases. Give it a shot for a different approach than we talked about earlier in the book!

Instructions

Felt the Wool

Fill your slow cooker halfway with water and add a teaspoon of liquid dish-washing detergent. Then turn the slow cooker's dial to the High setting. (If you don't have a slow cooker, or just don't feel like extracting yours from the deep recesses of your kitchen cabinetry, heat some water on the stove and then pour it in a bowl with a teaspoon or so of dishwashing liquid. Add more hot water as needed to maintain a hot bath.)

While the slow cooker is heating, pull tufts of fleece from your roving. Spread the fleece out on your work surface, laying it in a thin, even layer that is approximately the size of your hand. Over this layer, lay a new layer—this time in the opposite direction. Continue adding layers until you have 4 or 5.

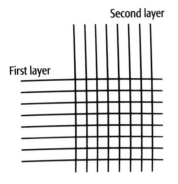

Second layer

First layer

Layer your fleece in opposite directions.

arefully pick up your fleece layers and gently rub them between your palms just enough to lightly mat them but taking care to ensure they don't roll.

unk the mat into your hot water bath for a few seconds.

sing tongs, pull the mat back out of the pot (don't be concerned if, at this point, it resembles your Uncle Ernie's toupé more than it does felt). Let some of the hot water drain off and, making sure not to burn yourself, rub the mat once more between your palms. If it gets too sudsy, rinse it in warm water.

ub the mat gently and dunk it until you have an even and thin—but sturdy—layer of felt, approximately the size of your palm.

ay the felt on a kitchen towel and let it dry overnight.

Construct Your Earrings

sing a penny as a template, cut out four pieces of felt, two fronts and two backs.

arefully stitch your design, staying at least ¼-inch away from all edges.

ay one unstitched piece of felt on your foam block and cover it with a stitched piece, face up.

sing your felting needle, carefully stab the unstitched portions of the earring, avoiding the areas with the stitched motif. Move the needle in a straight-up-and-down fashion, making sure you repeatedly shove it through both layers of felt. Note that you're not sewing here, just piercing the felt; felting the two pieces in this manner will fuse them together.

hen the two layers of the earring have been joined, use your felting needle to repeatedly pierce any portions that aren't smooth. The up and down motion of the felting needle will meld the fibers together more tightly and will smooth the area.

epeat the previous three steps with the front and back of the other earring.

hread one strand of very dark mocha brown embroidery floss (DMC 3031) on your needle.

ush the needle into the side of the earring, then up through the center of the top. Draw the needle and thread through the earring until about 3 in. of the thread's tail is sticking out the side.

apture the jump ring, thread it onto the top of the earring, and tie a knot.

oop your thread through the jump ring and the earring several more times; then tie one more knot.

ush your needle back through the piece from the top near the jump ring out the opposite side of your piece from where you started.

ut the excess thread on both sides of the earring to conceal both the starting end of the thread and the tail.

epeat the previous six steps to attach the second earring and jump ring.

Finishing Instructions

ttach these loops to ear wires; now you have a set!

Variation

by Roxane Cerda

You can use this same technique to make a fabulous pendant. To do so, just follow the preceding steps and then the ones below.

Project Rating: Flirtation

Cost: $20

Necessary Skills: Embroidery; needle felting (page 47)

Materials

- 100 percent wool roving (We chose a variegated brown for ours.)
- Slow cooker or large bowl
- Dish soap
- Kitchen towel
- Kitchen tongs
- Shears
- Embroidery scissors
- 1 skein brown (DMC #3031) embroidery floss
- 1 skein ivory (DMC Ecru) embroidery floss
- Embroidery needle, size 5
- Felting needle
- Beading needle, size 10
- Foam block
- Approximately 12 size 11 delica seed beads in colors that complement embroidery floss
- 24 inches of 3mm faux suede cord
- 1 6mm sterling silver closed jump ring
- 2 8mm large bore bone beads
- 2 4mm large bore bone disk-shaped beads
- 2 2mm large bore wooden beads

continued

continued

Create the Pendant

Trace the shape provided here onto a piece of paper and cut it out. You'll use it as a template to construct the pendant for your necklace.

Trace this shape for the pendant.

Using the template, cut two identical pieces of felt. (If you'd rather use a different shape, have at it! Just make sure you wind up with two identical pieces of felt.) Thread your needle with two strands of ivory embroidery floss and, using a straight satin stitch, stitch the design provided here. Be sure to leave a quarter inch margin of unstitched felt around the perimeter of the pendant.

Thread your beading needle with one strand of brown embroidery floss and, where indicated, use small half cross stitches to stitch on the beads.

Snip all thread ends on the back side of the pendant so they're less than $1/2$ inch long.

Using the same techniques as in the main project, join the front of the pendant to the back of the pendant and smooth out the edges. Next, using the same techniques as in the main project, attach the jump ring to the top of the pendant.

Stitch the ivory thread.

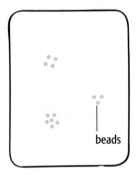

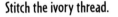

beads

Add the beads.

String the Necklace

Tie a knot at the end of your suede cord. String-in this order-a 2mm bead, an 8mm bead, and a 4mm bead.

Tie a second knot just above the 4mm bead to secure the three beads you just added to the end of the cord.

Slide the pendant onto the necklace using the jump ring at the top of the pendant.

Tie a third knot approximately 2 inches from the opposite end of the suede cord; then string a 4mm bead, an 8mm bead, and the remaining 2mm bead.

Tie a final knot on the very end of the cord to secure this second set of beads and clip the end of the cord to match the opposite end. The result is a leather strand with some beads at each end.

Making the necklace.

Tie the cord jauntily around your neck. A necklace you have!

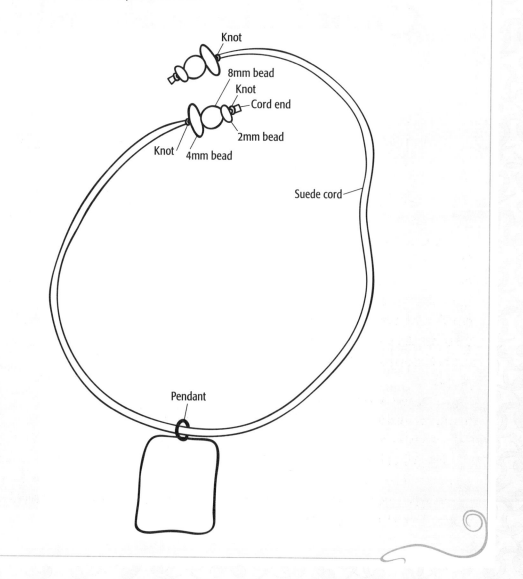

Knot

8mm bead

Knot

Cord end

2mm bead

Knot   4mm bead

Suede cord

Pendant

Chapter Nine

◆◆◆

Cozy Felt for Your Home

Felted Soapy Blue Balls

Your favorite soap, jazzed up with a scrubby wooly cover.

Get Off Your Felted Soap Box

Store your soap balls in style with this cute fulled box.

Who Needs Flowers? Vases for Crafters

Crochet and needle felt sturdy wool tubes for storing knitting needles, crochet hooks, and other notions.

Rainbow Bridge Baby Blanket

For a special baby in your life, this gently fulled blanket is a work of art.

Octopillow

Using a tie technique inspired by Japanese Shibori, an old sweater is given a stunning new life.

Felted Soapy Blue Balls

by Kathy Stowell

As a soap maker, I've noticed people tend to love soap balls! The shape seems to make the soap easier to fondle and grope. The felt covering behaves as a built-in washcloth as well as dresses up the soap pretty for your next shower date!

Project Rating: Flirtation

Cost: $7

Necessary Skills: wet felting balls and beads (page 26)

Finished Size

One bar of soap makes approximately two felted soapy blue balls measuring three in. in diameter.

Materials

- Bars of high-quality handmade soap shredded up via a cheese grater (or buy some pre-shredded from your local soap maker!)
- Merino wool roving in various shades of blue, approximately 1 generous handful per soap ball
- Spray bottle
- Cookie sheet
- Wire rack
- Mixing bowl large enough to fit your hands comfortably
- Rubber gloves

Instructions

Lay out your soap shreds onto cookie sheet. With a water-filled spray bottle, gently mist the shreds until slightly moist.

With gloves on, divide the shreds into hand-sized piles. Picking up a pile, begin to form the soap into a ball shape by squeezing, squishing, massaging, caressing, and anything else that just feels right. When you have a happy ball shape, place onto cooling rack to dry overnight. A sleepover if you will.

Next day: Fill the mixing bowl with hot water. Pick a shade of blue and with a thin layer of roving wrap your ball and then remove any excess tufts that remain. With that same shade, wrap another thin layer of roving around allowing the fiber to criss-cross the first coat. You shouldn't be able to see too much of the soap through the wool. If so, give your ball another layer of love for good measure.

ow, put your gloves on, for things really begin to get intimate. Hold your ball over the bowl and sprinkle drops of hot water lightly all over to slowly wet.

ext, agitate the fibers by gently rubbing the roving into the soap while sprinkling more hot water every once in a while (we want to keep things hot!).

inally, submerge your ball into the bowl for about two seconds, remove, and give it a good squeeze; then cool things off with a cold shower of gently running water.

Finishing Instructions

llow your ball to dry on the cooling rack. Half way into the drying period, rotate the ball and smooth out any grid marks with your fingers.

Variation

Sick of balls? Life's too short not to experiment! Swing the other way with the classic bar of soap! Just skip the shredding-and-rolling-the-soap steps. Or, try playing with layers of different colors for a marble look. This project is also a good opportunity to whip out your felting needle and design directly onto your felted masterpiece.

Get Off Your Felted Soap Box

by Kathy Stowell

In case the sighting of blue balls lounging in the bathroom elicits unwarranted gossip, let this box do the explaining. As well as keeping all of your balls in a row, the word "soap" needle-felted in should spell it out to inquiring minds.

Project Rating: Flirtation

Cost: $12

Necessary Skills: basic knitting (page 191); needle felting on a flat surface (page 47); fulling in the machine (page 50)

Techniques:

K2tog Knit the next two stitches together as one.

M1 Make one stitch by inserting the left needle, from front to back, under the horizontal strand of yarn between the stitch just knit and the next stitch, and knitting it through the back loop.

I-Cord Using a double-pointed needle, CO required number of sts; Next Row: Instead of turning work around to work back on the WS, slide all sts to other end of needle, switch needle back to your left hand, bring yarn around back of work, and start knitting the sts again. I-Cord is worked with the RS facing at all times; Repeat this row to form I-Cord. After a few rows, work will begin to form a tube.

Finished Size

Length: 3.5 inches
Width: 3.5 inches
Height: 3 inches

Materials

- MC: Morehouse Farm Merino 3-Strand (140 yd/128m per 57g/2oz skein, 100 percent Merino wool); Color: Soft Pink–1 skein
- CC: Cascade 220 (220yd/200m per 100g/3.5oz skein, 100 percent wool); Color: #9740–1 skein
- Substitution: Approx. 33 yd/30 m worsted weight feltable wool for MC, and 22 yd/20m for CC. Two different yarns were used for the sample box. If you also wish to use two different yarns (instead of two different colors of the same yarn), consider knitting and fulling a swatch to ensure that both yarns full at the same rate.
- 1 pair US 10.5 / 6.5mm straight needles
- Two US 10.5 / 6.5mm double-pointed needles
- US G / 4mm crochet hook
- Wool roving for needle felting
- Felting needle

Gauge

14 stitches = 4 inches/10cm

Instructions

Main Piece (Sides and Bottom)

Using MC and straight needles, CO 22 sts.

Work 2 rows in stockinette st, beginning with a RS row.

Decrease Row [RS]: K1, k2tog, k to end.

1 row.

Repeat these 2 rows 7 times more. 14 sts remain.*

Next Row [RS]: P all sts. This row marks the folding line between the first side and bottom of the box.

Continue in stockinette st until work measures 4 inches from folding line, ending with a WS row.

Next Row [RS]: P all sts. This row marks the folding line between the bottom and second side of the box.

1 row.

Increase Row [RS]: K1, m1, k to end.

1 row.

Repeat these 2 rows 7 times more. 22 sts.

1 row. BO all sts.

Sides (Make 2):

Work from beginning to * as for sides and bottom.

BO all sts.

Finishing Instructions

Assembly

Note: All seams are made by working single crochet through the edges of both pieces being attached, using CC.

Match short (bound-off) ends of side pieces to side edges of box bottom, then fold sides of main piece up so that side edges of box sides meet. Crochet around all edges to join. Work 1 row sc around top edge of box.

Using CC and double-pointed needles, CO 4 sts. Work a piece of I-Cord long enough to fit around bottom edges of box. Sew in place. Weave in all ends.

Full box according to directions in chapter 4 until desired size and density is achieved.

Place box upside-down over a small box or crumpled paper to help it retain its shape while drying, and allow to dry completely.

se roving to needle felt the word "Soap" on the side of the box, following directions in chapter 3.

Who Needs Flowers? Vases for Crafters

by Amy O'Neill Houck

Recently, I saw some beautiful rubber knitting needle vases, and that got me thinking . . . I love crocheting containers, and fulling makes these vases strong enough to hold all your needles and notions. Once you get the hang of the basic concept, you can make containers in every size to hold things all over your house! Although it probably goes without saying, if you want to use these for flowers, make sure to stick a glass vase inside the wool one; wool is water resistant, but won't actually hold water!

Project Rating: Flirtation

Cost: $10-15

Necessary Skills: ch (page 186), sc (page 187), hdc (page 188), sewing ends (page 194), fulling in the machine (page 50), needle felting on a flat surface (page 47)

Finished Size

Before Felting

Diameter: 4 inches

Height: 5[10] inches

After Felting

Diameter: 3 inches

Height: 4[8] inches

Materials

- [MC] Cascade 220 Heathers (100g, 220 yd/ 201m, 100 percent wool), Color: #2445; 1 skein
- [CC] Cascade 220 (100g, 220 yd/ 201m, 100 percent wool), Color: #2450; less than 1 skein
- Substitution: Worsted weight feltable wool: approx. 110 yd/100m of MC and less then 20 yd/18m of CC (used for needle-felted surface design) are required. Ball band will indicate a gauge of approx. 20 sts = 4 inches in stockinette st.
- US K /10.5 / 6.5mm crochet hook
- Safety pin or split ring marker
- Felting needle and grip for single needle felting. We used Colonial Felting Needles Blue Point (36 gauge) and Blue Grip
- A foam pad for needle felting, cut to fit inside fulled vase. Read all about it in chapter 3.
- Tailor's chalk
- Yarn needle
- Sharp fabric scissors

Gauge

Since these vases are worked in the round, the pre-felting dimensions are more important than an accurate gauge; just be sure that you have a pliable, loosely worked fabric. Shrinkage of approx. 30 percent can be expected during felting.

Instructions

Note: Vase is worked in a spiral. Place a safety pin or split ring marker in the last st of the round to help you keep your place.

Base

sing MC, ch 4. Sl st in 1st ch to form a ring.

ound 1: Work 8 hdc into ring.

ound 2: 2 hdc in each hdc. 16 hdc.

ound 3: [Hdc in first hdc, 2 hdc in second hdc] 8 times. 24 hdc.

ound 4: [Hdc in first 2 hdc, 2 dc in third hdc] 8 times. 32 hdc.

ound 5: [Hdc in first 3 hdc, 2 dc in fourth hdc] 8 times. 40 hdc.

ound 6: [Hdc in first 4 hdc, 2 hdc in fifth hdc] 8 times. 48 hdc.

ontinue working as set, increasing 8 sts in each round, until work is 4 inches in diameter.

Sides

ound 1: Hdc in back loop of each hdc.

ound 2: Hdc in each hdc.

epeat Round 2 until work measures 5[10] inches from Round 1. Break yarn, draw through loop and pull tight.

Finishing Instructions

ull as directed in Chapter 4. The vases shown required 3 full wash cycles to full completely. Because these vases are small,

they won't be damaged by going through the spin cycle.

rim yarn ends and let dry completely. If desired, insert a drinking glass or other form into the vase while it is still wet, and let it dry around this form; this will help shape the vase.

se sharp scissors to trim top edge of vase if desired.

Needle Felting

se tailor's chalk to draw design on outside of vase. Insert foam into vase.

ay CC on vase following chalked design and needle felt in place, following directions in Chapter 3.

Variation

Scissors, Roving, and More Containers

Want to go crazy when you're trimming the top of your vase? Add a decorative edge, like a scallop-or use pinking shears to get a zigzag effect. When needle felting, you could also use a bit of roving to fill in your design (like the center of our grape leaves), or substitute roving for yarn.

If you want to make a different sized felted container, just continue building the base of your circle until it's about 30 percent bigger than you'd like your finished product to be, then stop increasing to build the sides. Remember, different yarns felt differently, so if you're substituting yarn, you'll want to felt a swatch before designing your own container.

Rainbow Bridge Baby Blanket

by Belinda Fireman

To celebrate a child's birthday at my children's school, the teacher tells the tear-inducing Rainbow Bridge story in which children are angels that cross the Rainbow Bridge to come to Earth before they are born. I made a version of this blanket to celebrate my son's birth. This blanket has two sides that are sewn together – it can tolerate twice the usual goobers and spit-ups!

Project Rating: Love o' Your Life

Cost: $130

Necessary Skills: basic knitting (page 191); fulling in the machine (page 50)

Techniques:

blanket stitch (Wrong sides of blankets face each other. Secure thread on inside, top left corner of blanket, and bring needle to back of work. Working from left to right, bring needle through both blankets, from back to front, but do not pull thread all the way through blankets. Draw needle up through the loop of thread which was formed, and pull to close loop. Create subsequent stitches in this manner to complete edging).

K2tog Knit next two stitches together

SKP Slip 1 st, knit next st, pass slipped stitch over stitch, just knit (as if binding off).

Finished Size

Before felting (each blanket):
Length: 31 inches
Width: 31 inches

After felting (each blanket):
Length: 26 inches
Width: 26 inches

Materials

- Noro Kureyon (50g, 111 yd/100m, 100 percent wool)
- **Uniquad Blanket**
- MC: Color #185–8 balls
  (Uniquad Blanket Substitution: Approx. 800m feltable worsted weight wool)
- **Multiquad Blanket**
- MC: Color #182–3 balls
- CC1: Color #95–2 balls
- CC2: Color #185–2 balls
- CC3: Color #153–1 balls
  (Multiquad Blanket Substitution: Approx. 800m feltable worsted weight wool)
- 1 set of 5 US #10.75/ 7mm double-pointed needles
- 1 24-inch/60 cm US #10.75/ 7mm circular needle
- Yarn needle
- Stitch holders
- 4-ply wool yarn or needlepoint thread

Gauge

Note: All gauge measurements given below are measured before felting. However, exact gauge is not important since the blankets will be felted, and the baby doesn't care what size it is!

Uniquad Blanket: 13–14 stitches = 4 inches in stockinette st on 7 mm needles

Multiquad Blanket: 12 stitches = 4 inches over small square pattern on 7mm needles
Each small square is approx. 4 by 4 inches, and each double square is approx. 8 by 8 inches.

Pattern Notes

Single Square

Divide 48 sts equally between 4 double-pointed needles and join to begin working in the round, being careful not to twist.

Odd-numbered Rounds 1–9: K all sts.

Round 2: [K2tog, k8, SKP] 4 times. 40 sts remain.

Round 4: [K2tog, k6, SKP] 4 times. 32 sts remain.

Round 6: [K2tog, k4, SKP] 4 times. 24 sts remain.

Round 8: [K2tog, k2, SKP] 4 times. 16 sts remain.

Round 10: [K2tog, SKP] 4 times. 8 sts remain.

Break yarn, draw through remaining sts and pull tight.

Double Square

Divide 96 sts equally between 4 double-pointed needles and join to begin working in the round, being careful not to twist.

Odd-numbered Rounds 1–9: K all sts.

Round 2: [K2tog, k20, SKP] 4 times. 88 sts remain.

Round 4: [K2tog, k18, SKP] 4 times. 80 sts remain.

Round 6: [K2tog, k16, SKP] 4 times. 72 sts remain.

Round 8: [K2tog, k14, SKP] 4 times. 64 sts remain.

Round 10: [K2tog, k12, SKP] 4 times. 56 sts remain.

Round 12: [K2tog, k10, SKP] 4 times. 48 sts remain.

Round 14: [K2tog, k8, SKP] 4 times. 40 sts remain.

Round 16: [K2tog, k6, SKP] 4 times. 32 sts remain.

Round 18: [K2tog, k4, SKP] 4 times. 24 sts remain.

Round 20: [K2tog, k2, SKP] 4 times. 16 sts remain.

Round 22: [K2tog, SKP] 4 times. 8 sts remain.

Break yarn, draw through remaining sts and pull tight.

Instructions

Multiquad Blanket

Note: Use the diagram and instructions for Single and Double Squares to make the blanket as follows. Use double-pointed needles, and always pick up sts with RS facing.

First Square

Starting in the upper left corner of the diagram, CO 48 sts using CC1, and make a Single Square.

Second Square

Using CC2, CO 36 sts, then pick up and knit 12 stitches along an edge of the first square. Make a Single Square.

Third Square

Using CC3, CO 72 sts, then pick up and k 24 sts along a long side of the rectangle formed by the first and second squares. Make a Double Square.

More Squares

Continue to make squares in this manner, following the diagram. The order in which the squares are knit is not important, but note that double squares are easiest to incorporate into the blanket by casting on 48 stitches (2 sides of the square), and picking up and knitting 48 stitches. Use the beautiful colors of Kureyon to your advantage; start in the center or outside of the ball, or break the yarn and start at a new spot in the ball to achieve your desired effect.

Garter Stitch Border

Note: pick up all sts for border with RS facing, using MC and circular needle.

First Side

Pick up and knit 94 sts along Side A of blanket.

K 7 rows. BO all sts.

Second Side

Pick up and k 5 sts along side edge of First Side, pick up and knit 94 sts along Side B of blanket. 99 sts.

K 7 rows. BO all sts.

Third Side

Pick up and k 5 sts along side edge of Second Side, pick up and knit 94 sts along Side C of blanket. 99 sts.

K 7 rows. BO all sts.

Fourth Side

Pick up and k 5 sts aling side edge of Third Side, pick up and k 94 sts along Side D of blanket, pick up and k 5 sts along First Side. 104 sts.

K 7 rows. BO all sts.

Weave in all ends on WS, using ends to close up any existing holes between the squares.

Uniquad Blanket

Note: This blanket is made up of 4 identical triangles.

Triangle (Make 4):

Using MC and circular needle, CO 88 stitches.

Row 1 (WS): P all sts.

ow 2 (RS): K1, k2tog, k to last 3 stitches, SKP, k1.

epeat rows 1 and 2, 25 times more. 36 stitches remain.

1 row.

ext Row (RS): K1, k2tog, k2tog, k to last 5 stitches, SKP, SKP, k1.

epeat these 2 rows 5 times more. 12 stitches remain.

1 row.

ext Row (RS): K1, k2tog, k to last 3 stitches, SKP, k1.

epeat these 2 rows 3 times more. 4 stitches remain.

1 row.

ext Row (RS): K2tog, SKP. Break yarn and place remaining 2 sts on hold on safety pin or stitch holder.

Note: If you want the stripes on the four triangles to match, try to start at the same location in the colorway, but note that not all balls are wound the same way. The yarn can be broken and reattached if necessary (especially if knots are found in the yarn).

hen all triangles are complete, sew them together along their diagonal edges, forming a large square with the held sts in the center. When the final edge is sewn, draw the sewing yarn through the 8 held sts and pull tight.

Garter Stitch Border

ork Garter Stitch Border as for Multiquad Blanket, EXCEPT pick up and knit 87 sts along each side, instead of 94 sts.

eave in all ends.

Finishing Instructions

ull both blankets at the same time, according to the directions in chapter 4. Check your progress frequently (approx. every 5 minutes). When blankets are sufficiently fulled (fuzzy, with stitches still visible, but not stiff!), allow them to run through part of the spin cycle and remove them promptly from the machine. Check that they are the same size. If not, one side can be felted more, or slight adjustments can be made when they are blocked.

lock the blankets by pinning them to a flat surface while they are still damp, and measure them to ensure they are the same size. Allow to dry completely.

ew the blankets together in the center, with wrong sides together. Sew the edges together using blanket stitch and 4-ply wool yarn or embroidery thread. Once sewn, soak the blanket in lukewarm water for 30 minutes, then pin it out to block it. Allow to dry completely before using; this may take several days.

Variation

Want a quick and easy project? Knit only one of the blankets. Want to do more? Knit the blanket larger and make a crib blanket/family heirloom! Don't feel like being straight and narrow? Allow yourself to "knit outside the lines" by ignoring straight edges–knit the squares at random for an irregularly-edged blanket. Or, try stuffing the blankets before sewing them up for an extra-large pillow. The uniquad blanket triangle patterns could also be made smaller by starting with fewer stitches.

Octopillow

by Shannon Okey

Shibori-inspired shaped felting couldn't be easier, and there's so much you can do with it! (See chapter 2 for more on Shibori.) While Japanese Shibori artists use different tyeing techniques to create color patterns when dyeing fabric, you can tie and secure a wool fabric to create texture after fulling. You can use a wide variety of household materials to form the suckers, and simple stitching with thread or yarn keeps everything in place. The best part of this project? No previous experience is necessary! Just hit up the thrift store for wool sweaters, track down some plastic bottlecaps, and you're on your way.

Project Rating: Summer Fling

Cost: Free to $60, depending on what supplies you already have, versus what you need to track down.

Necessary Skills: Steam dyeing (page 67); fulling recycled felt (page 61); felted Shibori (page 63)

Finished Size

The sample shown here measures as follows, but you can make pillows as small or large as you like—stitch together multiple sweater bodies for supersized, or use just the sleeve for a mini-pillow.

18 by 23, prefelting

16 by 12 inches, postfelting

Materials

- One or more wool pullovers (as low as 50 percent wool will work, but for best results, higher percentages are better)
- Plastic bottlecaps in a variety of sizes. Expect to use at least 20.
- Cotton or other non-felting yarn
- Pillow form or polyfill (Don't buy your form until after the piece has been felted! Sizes may change drastically.)
- Needle and coordinating thread (can also use embroidery floss or contrasting yarn for extra color)

Optional:

To overdye fabric:

- Acid dyes
- Dyeing equipment, recommended in chapter 5

Instructions

Cut the top off your sweater of choice at the underarm line. You will have a large tube. For example, the tube created to make the pillow in the color photo was 18 in. across and 23 in. high before felting. You can overdye it now if desired or after felting (as Shannon did). For complete dye instructions, check out the information in chapter 5.

Tie sucker shapers as desired across the pillow's surface—you can use as many or as few as you like! To tie each sucker-shaped section, hold a bottlecap under the (unfelted) sweater surface, stretch the wool tightly across the cap, and tie it firmly beneath the cap using cotton yarn or another unfeltable twine. If you prefer inverted bubbles, tie the pieces with the caps on the public side.

Run the piece through one or more hot/cold cycles in your washing machine, depending on how quickly it felts.

Dry the piece in your dryer, or allow to air dry. Shannon recommends the dryer because she finds it makes the felting surface more even. If you do place the piece in the dryer, make sure that the pillow form or stuffing is safe for a hot dryer.

Cut the cotton pieces that are holding the bottlecaps in place and remove the caps.

To make the tentacle-y bubbles, push down the center of the raised, cap-shaped portion and stitch around its base with thread, embroidery floss or yarn. Repeat for each. You can also press the bubbles down flat and stitch around them in a circle for 3-D polka dots, or sew down only one side of the bubble to the felted base surface. Experiment! Mix and match! No matter what you do, it will look great.

When you are satisfied with the surface, turn it inside out and sew the bottom edge of the tube closed. If you are inserting a pillow form, turn the tube inside out, place the form inside, and stitch closed. If you are using polyfill, stitch one third of the right and left sides of the top edge closed, turn the tube inside out, and fill; then stitch the remaining center one third closed.

Finishing Instructions

If you like, you can also needle felt additional colored wool fiber inside the tentacles, or embroider with yarn around them. Do this before you stuff the pillow, however!

Variation

Creating texture on a fulled fabric just begs for experimentation. For example, Shannon's been working on an octopus coat made from an old wool duster sweater. She took the hood and arms off before felting and sewed them back on afterward . . . there's nothing more annoying than a felted sleeve!

Why not just felt the sleeves with the sweater? In addition to the chance that a sleeve may felt together, or shrink into a blood pressure cuff, it's also nice to have a more flexible fabric for the sleeve sections. Having elbows that bend tend to come in handy!

Scarves are another good choice for shibori-inspired tying prior to felting, For shapers, don't limit yourself to bottlecaps. You can use just about anything as a shaper if it can go through the washer without damaging it—how about rubber bouncy balls? Or square erasers? As long as it will hold its shape in water, you can use it.

· Part Three ·

History and Resources

Chapter Ten

◆◆◆

A Brief History of Felt

Older than your grandmother, older than knitting, and even older than weaving, the act of making felt from raw wool is the most ancient textile art. Before felt-making, your average teenage girl was forced to wear fur to cover up! That's right. As the first type of man- (and woman-) made fabric in the history of the world, wool (and cashmere) felt quickly became the style for cavegals in the know.

Since we're talking about a time that long predates books, writing, and even cave cartoons, the origins of felt are pretty hazy. However, historians and textile artists have some good guesses.

See Jane. See Jane Felt.

Let's say a lovely nomadic girl, Jane, is foraging out in the bushes of Mongolia for some tasty berries. She sees a bit of fluff on one of the bushes. Not at all unusual; the sheep back then (as they do now) used the branches as back scratchers, particularly during the time of the year when they shed their thick coats. She takes a handful of the fleece. It feels warm and soft. Suddenly, she remembers how her camel-skin stilettos cause unsightly blisters on her heels. What if she lined them with this fluffy stuff? That would probably feel good after a long day of foraging!

So, Jane fills her uncomfy shoes with wool one morning. She gathers berries all day and is grateful that her feet aren't complaining as loudly as usual! When she gets home to her *ger* tent that night, she watches her sisters rubbing their sore toes. Always one to show off, Jane pulls off her own shoes to show them the wooly fluff.

She's surprised that the fluff has been pressed and matted into a strong and soft cloth, just the shape of her foot!

As Jane's sisters gasp in wonder, Jane imagines scores of uses for this new discovery. She could create lightweight hats that wouldn't spoil a nice hairdo. She could sew stylish dresses, certain to woo that cute boy from the next camp over. She could line the walls of their *ger* with this fabric; surely it would help keep out the cold wind and wouldn't weigh as much as the furs they had been using.

Mongolian lamb.

Legends and Heroes

Of course, other myths are everywhere about the origins of felt. They seem to largely be associated with some guy 2,000 or more years ago. Some stories say that Noah, of the famed ark, discovered felt after lining the hull of his ship with fleece. When the animals all disembarked at the end of their cruise, Noah found that the fleece had been trampled into a fine carpet. Others credit St. Clement to the discovery, saying that he stuffed some wool in his hat and sandals when he went on the lam from his enemies some 2,000 years ago.

Scholars generally believe that our little story about Jane is close to the real scoop. Because of the flocks of wild sheep and goats, as well as the harshness of the climate, it's most likely that felt first developed in Central Asia, between 8,000 and 12,000 years ago. As the nomadic families traveled, they spread the art to other areas of the continent.

The first evidence of felt dates back to 6,000 BCE in Turkey, with some really fantastic and complicated artifacts found in burial tombs in the Altay Mountains of Siberia. Preserved by the ever-present permafrost, these artifacts included rugs, wall hangings, and decorative objects that pretty much prove felt-making was a sophisticated and evolved art at 600 BCE.

Mongolian sheep and goats.

Old, but Not Passe

Just like we discovered way back in chapter 2, the art of hand-crafting wool felt is pretty straight-forward. In fact, not much has changed since its origins. Even today, families in Central Asia still use the ancient techniques to create wool felt.

In Mongolia, felt is still used to line the insides of the round *gers* (see photo) that nomadic families use for houses and barns. As a decorative art, complex felt blankets and wall hangings use traditional symbols and motifs to tell stories.

Mongolian gers.

Elsewhere in the world, felt has traditionally been used for warm but lightweight hats, boots, and other garments. Of particular interest to fashionistas . . . hats made from the felt of beaver or rabbit fur were in high style in the eighteenth century. As machine processes took over many aspects of the textile industry, the fur was often replaced with less expensive and more common wool. For a macabre version of that hat story, check out the "Mad as a Hatter" sidebar.

Mad as a Hatter

Remember Lewis Carroll's *Alice in Wonderland* and the delightfully crazy Mad Hatter character? More than just a funny guy, the phrase "Mad as a hatter" has long been used as a colloquial description of insanity. Did you know that this actually relates to a felting process? In the eighteenth and nineteenth centuries, when those fur felt hats were in the height of fashion, the felting process included washing the pelts in a mercury solution to at once separate the fur from the hide and felt the fur together.

Of course, mercury isn't the best thing to work with, or even come close to. The combination of the toxic mixture and the vapors that were produced would poison the hatters, among other things, causing them to go a little bit insane.

But, don't worry about being afraid of your local hat maker. Thankfully, the use of mercury for felting was banned in 1941.

Modern Applications for Wool Felt

Even in cultures where handmade wool felt is overlooked, machine-manufactured wool felt has a vital part to play in life. Do you play piano? Even on new pianos, the hammers are made from wool felt. Are you a shark at pool? Your table is probably lined with pure wool felt. Even pens and tennis balls use machine-made felt.

Enviro-girls and guys may be interested in knowing that gigantic wool *mops* are being investigated as a safe and biodegradable way to clean up oil spills.

If you've tried out a few of the wet felting projects earlier in this book, you may be wondering where to buy a felt-making machine. These babies can be found on the wonderful Internet, but they start at more than $1,000 for a machine that can produce 28-inch sheets of felt. They work much the same way as when you make felt by hand . . . by rolling the fiber back and forth through a press-like structure. Of course, even with a machine, you'll still have to build all those layers of fiber yourself.

Getting your Fill of Fulling

Creating a felt-like fabric by deliberately shrinking a wool fabric developed much later in the grand scheme of things. The first fabrics (after felt, of course) were woven. Historians believe the first looms for weaving were developed around 6000 BCE. Of course, I like to think that the first fulling was a complete and total accident. Say, a careless husband trying to wash his wife's favorite woven tablecloth.

However, like many happy accidents, that same thick, water repellant fabric was discovered. Since the thickness of the felt-like fabric is determined largely by the thickness of the weave, suddenly drapey, fashion-worthy felt was possible. Instead of building up thin layers of fleece; a time-consuming and, as you can probably attest, stressful process, machines could be used with wool yarn to weave sheets of fabric that were then washed and dried. Et voilà! Felt!

Across Europe in the Middle Ages, *fulling mills* were established. These factories would use water power to roll and agitate lengths of woven cloth. The fulled cloth could then be sewn into clothing, hats, shoes, blankets, and more.

One of the most famous examples of fulling, at least in Canada, is the Hudson Bay Company Point Blanket. These warm wool blankets were introduced to the fur trade in 1779. The *points* on the blanket refer not to what the blankets were worth, but the size of the finished fulled blanket. The woven blankets were so popular that in the nineteenth century, additional mills had to be hired to weave and full the blankets. Some were even turned into apparel; sewn coats that were warm enough for the chilly Canadian winters. In the twentieth century, these blankets deviated from the traditional colors of yellow, green, and red on a white background. Today, you can still purchase Point Blankets at The Bay, the modern department store of the Hudson Bay Company.

Knitters Get into the Swing of Things

The question as to when knitters began to deliberately full their handwork is a bit tougher to answer. Some cultures in which traditional knit mittens were essential parts of daily life may have valued hand fulling as a way to increase the warmth and water resistance of the mittens. For example, some research shows that knitters in the Faroe Islands, halfway between Scotland and Iceland, have traditionally fulled finished mittens before wearing. However, because the budget of this book doesn't really allow for travel to exotic locales for the sheer purpose of research, I wasn't able to turn up a date range when this tradition may have began.

Suffice it to say, however long (or short) the tradition of fulling knitwear, the past five years have seen a massive amount of interest in the craft. The new trend began with bags. Knit a really large bag and shrink it in the washing machine. It even sounds fun! And, the finished fabric so little resembles knitting that non-yarn-lovers would be astounded and delighted. "You made that? But, how!?!?"

Today, doing a search on the Internet for *felted bag pattern* will turn up many more results than *fulled bag pattern*. For example, a recent search on Google turned up more than 10,000 hits for *felted bag pattern*, and only two for *fulled*. This shows the shift of language through this last batch of knitters.

I wish I had a definitive answer as to why the traditional definitions of *felting* and *fulling* have been shifting and becoming more loose, especially in the last decade. However, it may be as simple as *felted bag* is easier and more fun to say than *fulled bag*.

Whatever the case, fulling knitted items seems to be a trend with longevity. Although this book is one of only a few to cover all aspects of felting and fulling, your local bookstore will stock quite a number of books devoted to felting knitted things. And, most of the knitting and crochet magazines regularly feature felted bags, hats, mittens, and even garments.

Felt in the Mainstream

Although hand-felted items will likely never again be viable for the mass production our society demands, like many other traditional arts, felting and fulling seem to be at the beginning of a renaissance. Interest in wet felting has grown particularly in the past few years. It's messy, and clever, and addictively fun. It's wild, and wooly, and primitive and completely different from any other textile art. As local yarn shops and art schools begin to feature wet felting courses alongside knitting and weaving, I can only hope that more craftaholics will give it a whirl.

After all, very, very cool things happen when new approaches are taken to old skills. I'm looking forward to seeing what the next decades will bring to the art.

Chapter Eleven

◆◆◆

Happy Procrastinations: Cool Felting Resources On-Line and On-Land

Welcome to the wonderful world of felting. Unlike knitting, sewing, or crochet patterns, where specific measurements, stitch directions, and shaping instructions are fully explained, patterns for wet and needle felting are quite a bit more freeform in nature, and as such, are perfect media for expressing your personality. Few crafts, therefore, are better suited to a little outside inspiration. This chapter isn't intended to be the be-all and end-all of all the felting information that's out there. Instead, use the included links and references as a jumping-off point. One other point to note; for more knitting- and crochet-specific references, you'll be best off to check out *Not Your Mama's Knitting* and *Not Your Mama's Crochet*, both by Wiley Publishing, Inc.

Stash Enhancing Fun

The crafter's stash is rarely more handy than when you're addicted to felting. Since wet felting a large object can take some serious set up and clean up time, it's great to be able to avoid a last minute trip to several stores to collect what you need.

Instead, consider putting together one of those felting kits recommended in chapter 1. Keep on hand your old towels, bubble wrap, plastic bags, tea kettle, and lots and lots of fiber, and you'll be set to go whenever you feel the felting whim.

Yarn Shops

Finding local sources for felting fibers and needle felting stuff can be tough. Although some of the larger mass-market yarn companies, such as Lion Brand and Patons, are now producing a 100 percent wool yarn for fulling, natural feltable yarns can be tough to find in the big box chain stores. And, at the time this book was written, none of the chains stocked any fiber or needle felting equipment.

So, you'll need to venture beyond your local mall and into some indie shops to find what you need for this books' projects.

Trying on a LYS for Size

If you're new to knitting, or haven't stepped much outside the big box craft stores, your first visit to a *local yarn shop* (LYS) may be surprising. You'll find yarns of all fiber contents and most price ranges, from $4 a ball to $50 or more for the finest cashmere.

These shops can usually be found in areas of town that cater more toward independent retail shops. So, you'll be unlikely to find a LYS in a mega-mall. For an idea of where to start looking, check out your local business directory. Look under *Wool-Retail* and *Yarn-Retail* for a place to start. Depending on how your local stores describe themselves, one or the other headings will likely work. Also, check out the shop listings on WoolWorks (www.woolworks.org). Although the site is manually updated, and may not be entirely up to date, it does feature quick blurbs about each shop, as well as the standard contact info. Finally, do a Web search for yarn shops in your city.

Every yarn shop will have a different feel. Some may be instantly warm and welcoming. Others will expect you to ask the questions and will let you browse at your leisure. If one shop doesn't feel like a good fit for you, don't get discouraged. Try another store, if you can. Or, just go back on a different day. Remember that although there's never a good excuse for bad customer service, yarn shop employees sometimes have bad days, just like everyone else.

What You Can Expect

For more patterns for felted bags, local yarn shops are a great place to start. Most stock good selections of these trendy and fun projects and can get you going with suitable yarns. In any case, don't be afraid to ask questions! Curious as to whether a certain yarn will felt? Go ahead and ask for advice. Most shops will be able to quickly identify several good yarns for felting projects.

Outside of yarn, supplies for wet and needle felting can be harder to track down, but even this has been changing. As the craft of hand spinning has grown, a lot of yarn shops are beginning to stock more and more fiber for spinning, which means fiber for felting, too!

It's most common for shops that specialize in spinning to stock primarily natural colored fibers, such as what Suzen Green used in her "Subzero Scarf for the Urban Dweller" in chapter 7. But, if you're lusting after something a little more colorful, ask to be set up with some basic dye equipment and check out the instructions in chapter 5.

So, if your shop of choice doesn't even carry undyed merino fiber, why not ask and see whether it's in the plans?

Need to brush up on your knitting or crochet skills? Every yarn shop should offer frequent courses covering both basic techniques. Even if you know a little already, enrolling in a course can be a great way to make connections and get inspired, as well as picking up a few new tricks of the trade.

Other Great Local Sources

Depending on the selection at your local yarn shop, you may have to venture further-a-field to track down felting fiber, dyes, and equipment.

Quilting and Fabric Shops

Since needle felting can be done with high-end sewing machine attachments, many quilting and fabric shops sell small packs of dyed fiber for embellishments. These can also be handy places to pick up felting needles.

Fabric shops, particularly those devoted to fashion fabrics, are good sources for scissors, rotary cutters, and silk chiffon, such as used for laminate or nuno felting. Larger cities can also have a selection of fabrics for saris and other Asian garments. Don't miss these shops; you can find great bargains on all kinds of interesting silks!

Art School Supply Shops

Since many art schools now offer courses in fiber arts, the college bookstore can be a handy spot to pick up cheap fiber, dyes, and felting needles. Call first to see whether you need to be enrolled to purchase items.

On the Farm

No matter where you live, within a few hours' drive is probably some kind of farm or wool processing mill. These are fun day trips, where you can see some of the sheep, alpacas, or llamas and get great deals on often unprocessed fleeces. Many of these farms will also sell cleaned and carded fiber for spinning and felting.

Again, WoolWorks (www.woolworks.org) is a great first resource for finding sheep farms. But, don't forget to do a Web search, as you'll often find newer places to visit.

Online Stash Enhancement

Even if you live in the smallest community, if you have Internet access, you're connected to the biggest felting supply network in the world.

Shopping online has both ups and downs. On the plus side, you're likely to find better selection and lower prices. On the minus end of things, you'll have to wait for the delivery of any purchase, and you're unable to touch, feel, smell, and see the product clearly before purchasing.

Finding spots online to spend your hard-earned cash couldn't be easier. Most of the companies whose products we used in this book have Web sites that clearly list all shops stocking their products. Many also have provided links to individual store Web sites. Some even sell direct.

Guilds, Festivals, and Courses

Wet and needle felting are often labeled as *fiber arts*, and so can often be found alongside hand spinning and weaving offerings. If spinning courses or events are being promoted, check out the brochure . . . you may find some felting treats as well!

Guilds

Most communities have at least one Fiber Arts Guild. Sometimes these are catch-all groups, covering everything from embroidery, to knitting, to spinning, and weaving. In other cases, you'll be able to find a guild focused on only one or two arts. For a nominal membership fee, you can attend periodic meetings, guild retreats, and classes and sometimes even get discounts at local supply shops. Guilds are a great resource. You may be the youngest member, or the oldest, but you'll likely learn a lot from your fellow guild members.

Festivals

Local fiber arts festivals are often produced by a guild. Some of our local festivals in Calgary are held in surrounding community high schools on summer weekends. They feature courses, workshops, lectures, galleries, and fashion shows, as well as great marketplaces for vendors to show off their products.

For a wet felter, festivals geared toward spinners will be most helpful. After all, you'll probably see the widest variety of fibers all in one place! These festivals also sometimes feature classes.

Stitches East, West, and Midwest

Three times a year, XRX, the publisher of *Knitter's Magazine,* hosts consumer trade-shows. Featuring world-class speakers and instructors, plus a marketplace of hundreds of drool-worthy stalls, Stitches is, in many ways, the *crème de la crème* of yarn events. Watch their Web site at www.knittinguniverse.com for dates and exact locations.

Sheep and Wool Festivals

Wool and fiber producers attend sheep and wool festivals to promote their flocks, win awards, and interact with crocheters, spinners, and knitters. Although nearly every state and province has an annual wool festival, some of the most prominent include Salt Spring Island's Fiber Festival (www.fibrefestival.com), the Maryland Sheep and Wool Festival (www.sheepand wool.org), and the New York Sheep and Wool Festival, also known as Rhinebeck (www.sheepandwool.com). Most of the major magazines feature ads for the larger festivals. Smaller home-town fests may only be advertised in your local newspapers. If all else fails, check with LYS for details and dates.

Courses and Workshops

Outside of festival season and your local yarn shop offerings, check in with community colleges and art schools for extension course offerings. Non-credit classes are often held on evenings and weekends and are geared toward hobbyists as well as fiber artists. The variety offered can range from a few simple one-shot workshops to more complex and comprehensive courses ranging from Shibori dye techniques to laminate felting for sculpture.

The Wonderful World of Fiber Arts

As discussed in chapter 10, felting has been an established part of the serious art world for much of the past century. Felt artists can be found in most corners of the globe, creating spectacular and strange sculptures, wall pieces, miniatures, jewelry, and wearable art.

Exhibits of these works can be fun and inspiring. Check with your local galleries for listings of upcoming exhibits. You're probably best off sticking to galleries that focus on contemporary arts. Textile arts museums are a natural habitat for more permanent exhibits.

Publications

Outside of galleries and museums, two stellar magazines focus on fiber arts. In addition to just the information in the articles, the advertisers in these can give you a great place to start tracking down felting supplies.

Fiber Arts

Fiber Arts magazine focuses on all things fiber, from dramatic contemporary quilting to weaving. Profiles on exhibits and artists who work with felt are frequent, but as a crafter, I find that even the articles and photos of techniques I don't often use end up inspiring my work in other ways. For more information, check out www.fiberarts.com.

Selvedge

This exciting British periodical focuses on textiles and features spectacular photography, articles, and information. It can be hard to find, but a quick visit to their Web site at www.selvedge.org should give you a few places to start.

Felting Online

Even if you don't know a single other felter in real life, the Internet is a fab way to connect. Here are some ways to obtain patterns, be a blogger or a reader of blogs, and participate in felting forums and groups.

Patterns and Inspiration

Are you thoroughly addicted to fulling and felting? The Internet is an ideal source for patterns. Some are published by individual designers and are available free on Web sites or for a nominal download fee. Others are published as part of a magazine, such as *Knitty* (www.knitty.com) or *CrochetMe* (www.crochetme.com). Do a Web search for "felting pattern," and you'll turn up hundreds of options for fulling from knit or crocheted items. For wet felting patterns or inspiration, try searching for "wet felting" and see what turns up.

Blogs and Web Rings

For online inspiration, the best place to start is with the message boards and millions of blogs devoted to all things yarn. The Knitting Blogs Web ring, at last count, had well over 1,000 sites, most of which have completed at least one fulled project. You can access the ring homepage at boogaj.typepad.com/knitting_blogs, but most knitting blogs are also part of the ring navigation. Simply click Next to hop from one site to the next in line.

Online Forums and Groups

Knitters and crocheters will already be familiar with the huge forums at www.knittersreview.com/forum and www.crochetville.org. But, did you know that these forums feature special areas for felters? Also check out the felting-specific forum at feltingforum.com/phpbb/index.php. Many posters at all these forums include photos of projects or links to their individual sites for more information on their work.

Yahoo! Groups (groups.yahoo.com) is a seemingly endless collection of groups of all kinds. Do a search on groups.yahoo.com for *felting* and get grouping. Yahoo! Groups also makes it easy to start your own group on any topic you can dream up.

Get Connected: Start Your Own Blog!

Want a blog? With free online blogging software, it's easier than ever. Without knowing a lick of Web code, you can get set up and online within minutes. Check out these fully hosted sites for more information:

- ◆ Blogger: www.blogger.com
- ◆ Blogspot: www.blogspot.com
- ◆ Typepad: www.typepad.com
- ◆ LiveJournal: www.livejournal.com
- ◆ Xanga: www.xanga.com

If you already have a Web site and would like to start a blog, many Web hosts now include popular blogging software along with your hosting package. Check out some of these open-source favorites:

- ◆ GreyMatter: www.noahgrey.com/greysoft
- ◆ MoveableType: www.moveabletype.org
- ◆ WordPress: www.wordpress.org

When you're up and running, consider joining a Web ring to get noticed and get readers. Check out RingSurf, the Web's most popular ring system, at www.ringsurf.com.

Chapter Twelve

◆◆◆

Crocheting 101

Whether you already crochet and need a refresher or are looking for a place to start learning, this is the chapter for you! The hints and techniques on the next few pages should be plenty to get you hooking on the great crochet projects in Part 2.

If you haven't previously worked with yarn, crochet is a great place to start. With only one tool—a hook—and a bit of yarn, you can create sturdy and interesting fabrics. One of the great bonuses of crochet is that few crochet patterns expect you to be an expert, or psychic. Because crochet is a bit freeform in nature, the patterns must be written explicitly as to what you need to do and when you need to do it.

The following information is meant to be a quick and dirty introduction to basic crochet techniques. Need more help? Why not check out *Not Your Mama's Crochet* (Wiley Publishing, 2006)? Instead of covering the basics in just a few pages, it's got a whole book's worth of knowledge and funky projects.

Common Abbreviations

Ch: Chain
DC: Double Crochet
HDC: Half Double Crochet
SC: Single Crochet
Sl St: Slip Stitch
TR: Treble (or Triple) Crochet
YO: Yarn Over

The Basic Stitches

Although they may seem mysterious, all crochet patterns are built upon a fundamental set of basic stitches. Learn these, and you'll be prepared to tackle even the most complex patterns!

Slip Knot

Most crochet patterns start with a slip knot, followed by at least a few chain stitches. This is called a *foundation chain.*

To make a slip knot:

1. Form a ring-sized loop in the yarn, with the part of the yarn attached to the ball crossed in front of the loose end.
2. Bring the yarn attached to the ball up and behind the ring-sized loop.
3. Use your fingers to pull the yarn through the loop. Tighten into a knot by holding the top of the loop with one hand and pulling on both ends with the other hand.

Et voila! A slip knot! Now, insert your crochet hook into the loop and pull on both ends to tighten. The loop should be just big enough to slide loosely along the body of the hook.

Chain Stitch

Once your slip knot is on the crochet hook, you're set to work a *chain stitch,* often abbreviated as "ch" in crochet patterns.

1. First, you'll need to set up the yarn by bringing it over your left index finger and using your thumb and middle fingers to hold the tail just beneath the slip knot. This allows the yarn to be taught between the slip knot and your index finger.

2. Next, with the hook against the yarn, rotate three-fourths of the way toward you.

3. With the hook facing downward, bring the yarn through the slip knot.

4. You've just completed one chain stitch.

Slip Stitch

A *slip stitch* can be used anywhere you need to move the working yarn or join pieces without adding any significant height to the work.

1. Being careful to keep the chain from twisting, insert the hook into the very first chain after your initial slip knot.

2. As with the previous stitches, rotate the hook to bring the yarn over.

3. Draw through both loops on hook to create one loop. It helps to use your thumb and index finger to hold the ring open while you do this. Otherwise, the ring tends to twist and make it difficult to join.

Single Crochet

After completing a series of chains, in many cases you'll need to work into the loops of the chain for the first row. Here, we'll work a row of *single crochet* stitches.

1. Insert the hook from front to back through one loop of the chain. If working the first stitch on any row, you'll need to skip the first chain and work into the second one. This is then called a *turning chain*. Rotate the hook to grab the yarn, as if chaining.

2. Now, pull the yarn through the ridge on the foundation chain, pulling up a loop that's more or less the same size as the one on your hook. Your hook now has two loops.

3. Rotate the hook again to grab the yarn and pull through both loops.

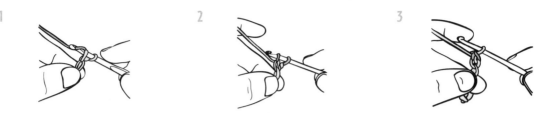

After you're past the first row of the piece, you'll be working into the top of a previous row instead of into the chain. The stitch is exactly the same. The only difference is that you'll instead put your hook through both "legs" of the stitch on the row below. See the illustration, right.

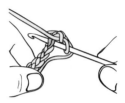

Double Crochet

The turning chain for a row of *double crochet* is usually 2 or 3 chains instead of 1, as with single crochet. Don't worry; your pattern will tell you what to do and won't expect you to know this by heart.

1. First, rotate the hook to grab the yarn. This is also called a *yarn over*.

2. Insert the hook into the next stitch and pull up a loop. You now have three loops on your hook.

3. Yarn over and pull through the first two loops, so that two remain.

4. Finish the stitch by yarning over and pulling through both remaining loops.

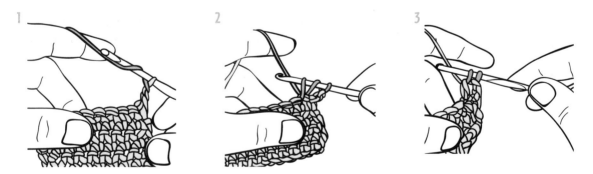

Half Double Crochet

1. First, rotate the hook to grab the yarn and then insert the hook into the next stitch and pull up a loop. You now have three loops on your hook.
2. Yarn over and pull through all three loops so that one remains.

Treble (Triple) Crochet

1. First, yarn over twice and then insert the hook into the next stitch and pull up a loop. You'll have four loops on your hook.
2. Yarn over and pull through the first two loops. Three loops remain.
3. Yarn over and pull through the first two loops. Two loops remain.
4. Yarn over and pull through the two remaining loops. One loop remains and you're set to work your next stitch.

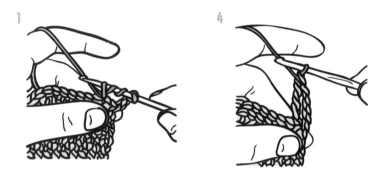

Working in the Round vs. in Rows

Working in the round is the official term for working in circles instead of turning the work back and forth when working in rows. You can just as easily crochet in circles. Most round work is begun with a foundation chain of just a few stitches that is joined with a slip stitch to make a loop. It's common to work your first round into the center of this loop rather than into particular stitches on the foundation chain.

Chapter **Thirteen**

◆

Knitting 1O1

Felting is the perfect medium for taking some chances with your knitting—so, you make a mistake or two along the way. Once the project is fulled, the mistake will be almost unnoticeable!

Chances are, if you don't already knit, you probably know someone who does. Knitting is at the forefront of the resurgence in home crafting. It's fun, not as hard as you'd think, and lets you craft cozy wearables.

The following information is meant to be a quick and dirty introduction to basic knitting techniques. Need more help? Why not check out *Not Your Mama's Knitting*? Instead of covering the basics in just a few pages, it's got a whole books' worth of information and cute crafty projects, including a fulled Techno Bag for your laptop.

Common Abbreviations & Definitions

K: Knit

P: Purl

K2tog: Knit two together

K1fb: Increase by knitting into the front and then the back of the same stitch

P2tog: Purl two together

Sl: Slip the next stitch from the left to right needle without working

St st: Stockinette Stitch; 1 row knit, 1 row purl when working back and forth. In the round, knit all stitches.

Tbl: through the back loops

YO: Yarn Over

The Basics

When knitting, you almost always move in a right to left fashion across the row of stitches. Stitches are made and then transferred, one by one, from the left needle to the right needle.

There are two main styles of knitting. In English or American knitting, the working yarn is held in your right hand and "thrown" around the needle to make a stitch. In Continental knitting, the working yarn is tensioned in your left hand, similar to crochet. The needle then picks at the yarn to make a stitch. Either method works perfectly well. The illustrations in this chapter are kept generic enough to make sense to both methods.

Use the following information and hints to help you work through the projects in this book.

Casting On

Putting stitches on your needles is called *casting on*. Here is how to do a basic Long-Tail cast on:

1. Pulling out a tail at least three times the width of your project, make a slip knot (see page 186 in chapter 12), and then place on a needle held in your right hand.
2. Next, use your left index finger and thumb to separate the two strands dangling from the slip knot.
3. Bring the needle down, creating a loop around the thumb. Insert the needle into this loop from bottom to top.
4. Use the left needle to grab the yarn that's extending around your index finger and pull back through the thumb loop.
5. Slide your thumb out to let go of the stitch. Get set up again as in figure 2 and repeat until you have the desired number of stitches.

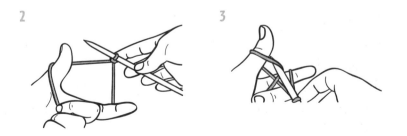

When you need to cast on in the middle of a row, you'll use the "Backwards Loop" cast on method. This is a simplified cast on that creates a very firm and non-flexible edge.

1. Make a loop out of the working yarn, similar to the beginning of the "Making a Slip Knot" instructions in chapter 12.
2. Place this loop on the right needle and pull on the end of yarn to tighten.

The Knit Stitch

1. First, with your yarn in back of the work, insert the right needle into the front of the stitch from left to right.
2. Next, wrap the working yarn around the right needle tip.
3. Finally, pull the right needle back out of the stitch, bringing the yarn with it to create a stitch on the right needle. Slide the previous stitch off the left needle.

Repeat across the row or as directed.

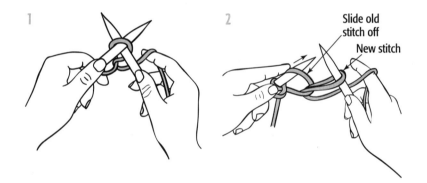

The Purl Stitch

1. First, with your yarn in front of the work, insert the right needle into the front of the stitch from right to left.
2. Next, wrap the working yarn around the right needle tip.
3. Finally, pull the right needle back out of the stitch, bringing the yarn with it to create a stitch on the right needle. Slide the previous stitch off the left needle.

1	2	3

← New purl stitch

Casting Off

This technique is also referred to as *binding off*.

To finish off a piece, you'll need to cast off. The most basic way works as follows:

1. Knit the first two stitches as usual. Insert the left needle into the *second* stitch from the tip of the right needle. See the figure below.

2. Use the left needle to lift this stitch over the other one and off the needle. One stitch has been cast off.

3. To continue casting off, knit the next stitch and repeat step 1. Since you only need two stitches at a time to cast off, after the initial stitches, you'll only need to knit one stitch, and then cast off one stitch.

Advanced Techniques

Of course, once you're comfortable with the basics, you can move on to patterns that ask you to do things like work in the round and picking up stitches. The following section introduces a few more of the techniques you'll need to complete the projects in this book. Anything specific to an individual pattern will be described in that pattern in sufficient detail.

Working in the Round

Knitting "in the round" usually creates a tube-like fabric that's perfect for socks, mittens, hats and more. Instead of knitting on two needles, back and forth in rows, you'll cast on over a set of 4 or 5 double-pointed needles, or use a circular needle with a bendy cable between two needle points.

While this is surprisingly easier than most new knitters think, there are a few pitfalls to keep an eye out for. When you join the cast-on stitches to begin working in the round, really make sure that the stitches are aligned straight on all the needles. For example, the cast-on edge should be facing the same direction everywhere, and should not be rotating around the needles. Another handy tip; use a stitch marker to note the beginning of your round. If you're using double-pointed needles, you won't be able to put the marker on the end of a needle; it'll fall off. Instead, place it one or two stitches in from the end of a needle. Getting spaces or "ladders" between two stitches where your needles meet? Focus on tightening up the first and last stitch on either side of that gap.

Luckily, with fulling projects, a few imperfections like this will be felted right out.

Picking Up Stitches

Some projects, including the Ah! Savasana yoga mat bag, will ask you to pick up stitches along the side of a previously knit section.

1. Insert your right needle into the stitch where you want to pick up another stitch.
2. Wrap the yarn around the needle as if to knit.
3. Pull up the loop of yarn.

I-Cord

I-Cord, sometimes called *Idiot Cord*, is an easy way to create a skinny tube of knitting using only two double-pointed needles. I-Cord is most often worked over 3, 4, or 5 stitches. Here are instructions for working a 3-stitch I-Cord. To make a wider tube, just cast on more stitches.

1. Cast on 3 stitches onto one double-pointed needle.
2. Knit the 3 stitches, but do not turn work. Instead, slide the stitches to the right end of the needle.
3. Repeat step 2 until cord is desired length.

Putting it All Together

For any of the projects in this book, you'll be fulling the knit item, and will therefore require fewer picky finishing techniques. However, you'll still want to loosely sew in any yarn ends to prevent unraveling in the wash. This can be as simple as weaving the yarn in one direction a few inches. You can also . . . gasp . . . *knot* ends together if you're planning on fulling the item. Any knots can be trimmed later.

To seam pieces of knitting for fulling, you can use a running stitch or an invisible seam technique. Because you're fulling, the look of the seam isn't important. Just be sure to use the same yarn as the body of the piece and sew it with an even tension. Your seams should not be buckling or creasing at all. Any tension problems will be exaggerated by the fulling. Use the same type and brand of yarn to make sure the seaming yarn shrinks at the same rate as the rest of the piece.

Chapter Fourteen

♦◆♦

It's All About the Magic

Few handcrafts seem more magical to me than felting. In no other does the finished product seem so far removed from the materials used.

Take a ball of fluff. Add some hot water and some soap. Rub a little. Roll a little. Flip over and repeat.

It sounds more like a recipe for the perfect pie crust, or a line dance, than a way to make a warm and wooly scarf. And yet, it works marvelously.

It's also slightly magical, the way you never know *exactly* what's going to happen. Sure, you can predict that by placing this much fiber, you'll have a fabric this thick, or that by knitting a 60-by-60-inch sheet, you may end up with a 4-foot square blanket. But, you will never know *exactly*. How will the fabric drape? Will it get nubbly? Fuzzy? Crimpy? Will I be able to see through it? Will it be too big, too small, just right?

I hope this book has shown you a trick or two, but more importantly, I hope it has inspired you to keep playing, to keep experimenting, to keep conjuring with wool and water.

Felting, whether wet, needle, or fulling, is all about experimentation. Every project is an experiment. There are few predictable results. When it doesn't work, you can end up with a spectacularly unfashionable creation.

But when it works, when it creates exactly what you wanted or something fabulous you couldn't have imagined, it's truly magic.

Designer Bios

Roxane Cerda Roxane dabbles in dozens of crafts, and since she can't stay focused on one thing for long, has ended up a Jacqui of All Trades, master of none. Nonetheless, when she does whip up something spiffy, she loves to share and hopes you enjoy her projects. Roxane began to craft ages ago, and has looked back only from time to time, to ensure that she's not trailing bits of string and dropping beads all over the place.

Dana Codding Dana works as a geologist and knitting instructor in Calgary, Alberta. She recently won an award for being the only person to ever knit on a particular geological field trip and enjoys freaking out her co-workers by knitting in her office at lunch. She's best known for repeatedly saying "Relax. It's just yarn," to her students.

Belinda Fireman Belinda blames her mother, Esther Budd, for her addiction to yarn. Even though Bel spent many hours in her mom's yarn store in the 1980s (oh, the angora!), she managed to avoid knitting until 2003 when she succumbed to the call of the needles. Belinda's knitting is supported by her husband (who drives during family outings to allow extra knitting time) and three children (who tolerate it so long as they frequently receive hand-knit toys). Bel is currently researching ways to knit while breastfeeding, without much luck.

Suzen Green Suzen is a fiber artist living in Calgary, Alberta. She was introduced to wet felting in art school and developed a deep love-hate relationship with the craft by felting a door mat that took more than eight straight hours to complete. She has used wet felting techniques to make garments, sculptures, and her own one-of-a-kind monster toys. Primarily a knitter, she enjoys shaking up knitting traditions through sculpture and performance art. Her work has been featured on Knitty.com and has been  exhibited throughout Canada. When she's not reading feminist theory and knitting sweaters for exercise equipment, she works as a yarn monkey at Make One Yarn Studio.

Karen Harper Karen lives in Calgary with her husband, the engineer; her son, the rebel; and her dog, the terrier. She works with yarn all the live-long day (at the best shop ever!), knitting and needle and wet felting. When she's not obsessing over her Pullip dolls, horror movies, and the UFC, she is trying to keep her house clean. You can find her and her knitting blog/complaining zone (http://stringtheoryknits.blogspot.com/).

Amy O'Neill Houck Amy is a writer and designer. She learned to crochet at the age of eight from her grandmother. In 2002, she formed a fiber cooperative with some good friends called Neighborhood Knits. The group sold knitted and crocheted scarves at art shows and independent clothing boutiques. Amy has taught crochet and knitting students from ages 6 to 76, and everywhere from libraries to yarn shops, classrooms, and trains. She now teaches in schools and yarn shops around Washington, D.C., and her  home, Takoma Park, MD. Amy designs crochet and knitting patterns for yarn companies including Blue Sky Alpacas, Be Sweet, and Curious Creek Fibers. She is a frequent contributor to *CrochetMe*, and her essay "No Bed of Roses" appears in *Hooked, A Crocheter's Stash of Wit & Wisdom*, published in 2006 by Voyageur Press. Amy also maintains a popular fiber blog called The Hook and I, which features patterns, tips, techniques, and book and product reviews (http://hookandi.blogspot.com). When she's not designing with fiber, you'll find Amy in the kitchen devising recipes. Her articles on food and nutrition have appeared in print and online publications including *VegNews, Vegetarian Baby and Child*, and in her culinary blog, The Comfort Kitchen (http://comfortkitchen.blogspot.com).

Cecily Keim Cecily fights the good fight, that of the apartment dweller attempting to felt in coin-op washers. Thanks to this little project, her desk is currently covered in a rainbow of plastic buttons, and she rather likes it that way. You can learn more about Cecily and whatever may be on her desk on a given day at www.SuchSweetHands.com. Cecily co-authored  *Teach Yourself Visually Crocheting* (Wiley Publishing, Inc.) with Kim Werker. You can also find Cecily demonstrating her designs on the DIY channel's *Knitty Gritty and Uncommon Threads*.

Cindy Kitchel Cindy is a crafter from way back: When she was six, her grandma taught her to knit and crochet as a way to keep her occupied and out of trouble. As a mother of two small kids and a worker-outside-the-home, she finds there's never enough time to execute all of the knitting, crocheting, felting, sewing, and quilting projects that are rambling around in her head, keeping company with all the lyrics from *Thriller*. Check out Cindy's blog, which sometimes includes craft progress and patterns, at http://slowishfood.blogspot.com/.

Mandy Moore Mandy lives in Vancouver, BC, with her small family of husband and cat. She is, among other things, the technical editor for Knitty.com, and she was the technical editor for *Big Girl Knits* (Potter Craft, 2006) and *Not Your Mama's Crochet* (Wiley, 2006). She enjoys crocheting and knitting, because they are engaging to both sides of her brain, and technical editing because she is a control freak. She honed her skills by working in yarn stores for several years as salesperson, teacher, and general know-it-all. She is a hardcore making-things evangelist and will probably try to convince you that you should try (crocheting, knitting, sewing, painting), too! You can find her online at yarnageddon.com.

Debora Oese-Lloyd Debora lives in Calgary with her very devoted husband, Patrick. He does all the cooking and errand running so that she has more time to knit and contemplate the mysteries of the universe. She is currently working with the statement, "The stillness is the dance," both in her knitting and her life. She really is trying to slow down but with being the art teacher at the local Waldorf school; meddling in the lives of her three grown kids, Cassandra, Zachary, and Archie; and all those yummy events and classes at Make One Yarn Studio, the dancing part is just too tempting.

Shannon Okey Shannon is the author of the Knitgrrl book series, *Spin to Knit*, and *Crochet Style*. She co-authored *Felt Frenzy*, which includes even more recycled felt ideas, and the inspirational thrift store sewing guide, *AlterNation*. Shannon has appeared on several crafty TV shows, such as *Knitty Gritty*, *Uncommon Threads*, and *Crafters Coast to Coast*, and writes/designs for many different magazines. She's also a city organizer for the indie craft festival Bazaar Bizarre. You can find her online at www.knitgrrl.com, via her shop Anezka Handmade (http://www.anezkahandmade.com), or on the road teaching. Shannon lives in Cleveland, Ohio, with partner Tamas Jakab and several furry creatures who love to nap in piles of pre-felted sweaters.

Kathy Stowell Since moving from the big city to a small rural village, Kathy has been spending her days doting on her adorable husband, Craig, and lavishly mothering her baby girl, Edie Tangerine. When time allows, she loves to get crafty with knitting projects, work on her sewing skills, and pipe-dream about one day being able to spin so she can raise sheep with a purpose on their six acres of paradise—the Horniman Ranch. To rake in the dough, she teaches yoga and is the Hempress behind Do Be  Clean Handmade Hemp Soap 'n Stuff (www.dobeclean.com). You can follow her nerdy adventures at her blog, www.whiletangerinedreams.typepad.com.

Becky Wright Becky has always been a part of the fiber arts community through the work of her mother and grandmother. She discovered jewelry a couple of years ago and has since been on a quest to design and produce unique, one-of-a-kind pieces under the name The Anna B Company. She's currently having the time of her life creating wonderful pieces and wonderful friendships through fiber arts and jewelry.

Index

◆◆◆

G

H

About the Author

Amy Swenson learned to crochet when she was still young enough to make blankets for her dolls. She promptly forgot everything about needlework until she turned 23 and suddenly fell back in love with the idea of creating fabric. Since 2003, Amy has developed and distributed her own line of original patterns for felting, knitting and crochet, IndiKnits (www.indiknits.com), which can be found in more than 120 shops across North America.

Amy is thrilled to have worked on several textile arts projects, including writings and designs for Interweave Knits, Knitty.com, "Knit Wit," "Big Girls Knits," "Stitch and Bitch Nation," "Knitgrrl," and "Knitting for Dogs." *Not Your Mama's Felting* is her second book-length publication, the follow-up to *Not Your Mama's Crochet* (September, 2006).

With her partner, Sandra Tiano, Amy owns and operates Make One Yarn Studio (www.make1yarns.com), a textile arts shop focusing on fine yarns and fibers for felting, knitting and crochet. Amy lives and designs in Calgary, Alberta, where she and Sandra are the proud humans of four cats who, thankfully, leave the yarn alone.

There's lots more in store with *Not Your Mama's*™ Craft Books!

Hip and savvy *Not Your Mama's* books are designed for confident crafters like you who don't need to start at the beginning and don't want to go back to basics and slave over every pattern and page. These books get right to the point so you can jump right into real projects. With easy-to-follow instructions plus hints, tips, and steps for customizing projects, you'll quickly have something to show for your efforts—fun, trendy items to add sass and class to your wardrobe or home.

0-471-97382-3

0-471-97381-5

0-471-97380-7

It's knitting with a trés chic attitude. Projects include Pirate Socks, Boot-i-licious (boot jewelry), Girly (a sexy cardigan), Macho Picchu (a man's sweater), Techno Bag (a laptop case), Pampered Pooch Pullover, Hearts & Stars (cushions), and more.

Creative crochet is in today! Patterns include an Uber-Femme Capelet, Pseudo Kimono, Daisy Chain Neck Warmer, When the Jeans Don't Fit (recycled denim rug), Straight-Laced Tank and Shrug, Wowie Zowie Eco-Tote, Crocheted Bling, two super-cute plush toys, and more.

Do the bling thing. Projects include Financial Freedom (recycled credit card necklace), Tough Cuff, Catch Your Own Bouquet ring, Tipple Rings (wine stem markers), Girls Gone Bridaled (a tiara), Security Anklet, push pins with pizzazz, and more.

All *Not Your Mama's*™ Craft Books
$14.99 US/$17.99 CAN/£9.99 UK • Paper • 240-264 pp.
$7 \frac{3}{8}$ x $9 \frac{1}{4}$ • Lots of illustrations and color photos

Available wherever books are sold.

WILEY
Now you know.
wiley.com